TEN INNOVATIONS

An International Study on Technological
Development and the Use of Qualified Scientists
and Engineers in Ten Industries

CHRISTOPHER LAYTON

Routledge
Taylor & Francis Group

LONDON AND NEW YORK

First published in 1972 by George Allen & Unwin Ltd

This edition first published in 2018
by Routledge
2 Park Square, Milton Park, Abingdon, Oxon OX14 4RN

and by Routledge
711 Third Avenue, New York, NY 10017

Routledge is an imprint of the Taylor & Francis Group, an informa business

British Library Cataloguing in Publication Data
A catalogue record for this book is available from the British Library

ISBN: 978-1-138-50336-6 (Set)
ISBN: 978-1-351-06690-7 (Set) (ebk)
ISBN: 978-1-138-47901-2 (Volume 28) (hbk)
ISBN: 978-1-138-47902-9 (Volume 28) (pbk)
ISBN: 978-1-351-06682-2 (Volume 28) (ebk)

Publisher's Note
The publisher has gone to great lengths to ensure the quality of this reprint but points out that some imperfections in the original copies may be apparent.

Disclaimer
The publisher has made every effort to trace copyright holders and would welcome correspondence from those they have been unable to trace.

ROUTLEDGE LIBRARY EDITIONS:
THE ECONOMICS AND BUSINESS OF
TECHNOLOGY

Volume 28

TEN INNOVATIONS

TEN
INNOVATIONS

An International Study on Technological
Development and the Use of Qualified Scientists
and Engineers in Ten Industries

by

CHRISTOPHER LAYTON

in collaboration with
CHRISTOPHER HARLOW
CHARLES DE HOGHTON

London
GEORGE ALLEN & UNWIN LTD
RUSKIN HOUSE   MUSEUM STREET

First published in 1972

ISBN 0 04 600002 X

Printed in Great Britain
in 10 point Times Roman type
by Alden & Mowbray Ltd
at the Alden Press, Oxford

Acknowledgements

This study was originally commissioned in 1968 by the Central Advisory Council for Science and Technology, who asked Christopher Layton to explore, for their benefit, some of the reasons why Britain appeared to be obtaining a poor return from its large investment in qualified scientists and engineers. Charles de Hoghton and Christopher Harlow agreed to collaborate with him in the study, and PEP to provide facilities for it. It developed into a comparative exploration of the degree of success, in a number of key areas of innovation, of British companies and competitors in the United States and on the Continent.

Initially the study was confidential to the Central Advisory Council; on this basis the companies visited were most helpful in providing a large amount of confidential information. At a later stage it was decided that it would be valuable for PEP to publish both the resulting general analysis and the case studies on which it was based.

This involved removing confidential material and reaching agreement with the companies on what might be published. In consequence, certain companies were omitted altogether from the published study, as were some controversial passages and judgements. A stimulating further examination and reassessment of several of the industries also became necessary. In the published version none of the lessons of the study have been lost, even though, occasionally, pieces of evidence have had to be removed.

Christopher Layton wishes to thank Lord Zuckerman and the Central Advisory Council for commissioning the work in the first place, and for their valuable criticisms and comments made on it in a number of sessions of the Council. Many busy people in industry in the USA, Europe and this country contributed precious time and thought to the study.

Special thanks are also due to the late Charles de Hoghton and to Christopher Harlow for their work in conducting the initial interviews with many of the companies. Christopher Harlow also contributed to formulating the project and Charles de Hoghton undertook a good deal of tedious work in corresponding with the companies to obtain their agreement on texts. Responsibility for the final result is Christopher Layton's alone, but his two collaborators did much hard work in the early stages. Thanks are also due to the various secretaries who typed and retyped texts and raw material.

Contents

Tables

Charts

Introduction

In 1966–67 the United Kingdom spent just over a third as much on research and development (R and D) as the European Economic Community (EEC). The expansion of technological education in the last decade now means that the proportion of the age group 20–24 in Britain which obtains some kind of first degree in science or technology at a university, or an alternative qualification at another place of higher education, is as high or higher than in any advanced country. As Table 1 shows, 270 in every 10,000 young British people obtained a degree-level qualification in science or technology in 1964, compared with 420 in the United States. If the large number of technologists who win Higher National Certificates is added on the British side, the British proportion is actually larger than the American, at least in technology. In pure science, and in management, the United States does much more, and a far larger proportion of young Americans take some kind of university degree in either arts, science or technology. All the same, both in total output of technologists and by expenditure on R and D, Britain is well up in the race.

Yet Britain's rate of economic growth has hitherto been lower than that in any other major industrial country. Output per man in manufacturing industry is little over one-third as high as in America. In 1963, turnover per man was of the order of £3,400 in British manufacturing, compared with some £9,000 per man in the United States.

Some of the reasons for these shortcomings are of a general economic character. Rate of investment, problems of industrial relations, size of market and so forth, all play major parts in conditioning economic performance. In this study we have concentrated in the main on asking a more particular question: have we been making proper use of the now large output of qualified scientists and engineers (QSEs) which Britain produces? Are they organized and distributed properly? In particular, are they contributing fully to the process of innovation, which means not merely inventing, but also developing and producing the results of inventions and bringing them to the market place? If not, what should be done to improve the productivity of our QSEs?

Much macro-economic analysis of the role of research and development has already been carried out. In our study we adopted a different method – that of exploring, by case studies, actual company behaviour. Our method has been to explore innovation in ten areas of industry by visiting, in each case, one or more British companies and comparing their performance with companies in the United States and Continental Europe. Our study has been complicated by the fact that it has been carried out at a time of change and progress in British industry. A number of the British firms we visited have become acutely conscious of the problems and needs described in this report and have initiated policies to meet them during the course of our studies. This is a portrait of industry in transition.

In Part 1 of this book we first summarize the results of our studies on the companies and then outline our conclusions on their use of QSES. The detailed case studies follow in Part 2.

Part 1
MANAGING INNOVATION
AND THE USE
OF QSEs

Chapter 1

MANAGING INNOVATION

Successful innovation requires, first of all, individuals and teams capable of successful research and development. Britain has an abundance of such teams. But in many of the industries we studied (e.g. numerically controlled machine tools, cars) we found that skilful initial invention in the research and development departments has been marred in the past by inability to achieve effective commercial exploitation, either at the production phase or in marketing. In motor vehicles, for instance, there was no sign of American superiority in invention, despite larger expenditure on research by the US automotive industry than elsewhere. The basic reason for higher productivity in the American vehicle industry lay in superior production planning and engineering, which made possible both rapid introduction of new models, higher reliability and constant improvements in plant productivity. It is in production and marketing that Britain needs more qualified scientists and engineers.

DIFFICULTIES IN TRANSFERRING TECHNOLOGY

The application of first-class analytical and engineering skills to production and marketing in British companies is not accepted as a top priority on a sufficiently wide scale. The structure of engineering training has, particularly in the past, led to a sense of 'class division' among engineers; consciousness of this has led many of them to consider that the highest professional standing is achieved only by getting to the 'purest' end of the innovation continuum, that is the R and D departments. To the extent that this concept of professionalism's being associated with 'pure' work still exists, it militates against the movement of QSEs from R and D to production and marketing.

Our studies showed that an important factor in successful innovation is the transfer of information from development to production; and here we found that there is no substitute for the movement of people, including highly qualified ones. In the 1920s, the Cincinnati Milling Machine Company, for instance, was unable to persuade its production people to accept hydraulic drives and controls until they themselves were brought into the development department. A major reason for the success of Pilkingtons' plate-glass process was that it was developed in the production plant. Texas Instruments systematically hives off cells of development engineers who have developed a product, to become a small production/profit centre of their own.

Even more important than good communications between development and production are communications between development and the market. This is of crucial importance, especially in the capital goods industries, and requires qualified scientists and engineers in both places. QSE salesmen can fulfil the function of selling the product effectively, demonstrating it to the customer and applying it to his needs. But, in the more advanced capital goods industries, they can also bring a vital feedback of technical information, which stimulates development and conditions the decisions on which development is based.

The extreme case of this need is integrated circuits and, in particular, large-scale integration where design must be based on the customer's own evolving product, say the logic of a computer. The same need is present in other capital goods industries. Increasingly, the effective machine tool firm is becoming the firm which can analyse a customer's production requirements in detail and work out the most economic technical solution to his entire plant needs in the form of a system of tools. Two British companies, Molins and Herbert-Ingersoll (the latter a joint venture between Alfred Herbert and the US firm, Ingersoll) have taken this point. The key questions, particularly in a difficult business climate, are whether they can grow fast enough and how soon they can actually make the philosophy pay. This new approach in machine tools is a key to great increases in productivity, not only in the machine tool industry, but also throughout much of the economy, offering a leap forward particularly in the economics of batch production. One can envisage machine tool consultants' emerging to play a useful part in the business of analysing customer needs and getting tools systems developed to serve them. But basically this is the task of the machine tool industry itself, and with one or two key exceptions, it employs hardly any graduate engineers in marketing at all.

In the chemical plant industry, we found that the more careful analysis of customers' future needs and the development of plant design to suit them accounted for the success of American companies compared with some British ones. The US chemical plant companies we visited absorb information about both the market and processes and then develop designs, which they can offer to the chemical companies

4

as alternative systems when the moment comes. One British company, by contrast, evidently feels it is sufficient to ask the customer what kind of plant he would like, and then offer to build it. The American competitor, who foresees the customer's needs and develops future solutions, is almost bound to win.

The same lack of will and skill in commercial exploitation is sometimes found in Britain at the level of the small individual technical entrepreneur. One young British ex-graduate of the Harvard Business School runs a highly successful business which specializes in providing risk capital to new technological enterprises. He finds any number of inventors who have interesting products to offer. But hardly any have thought out a strategy for developing, producing and marketing the product.

THE ROLE OF THE SMALL ENTERPRISE

The best conditions for innovation are nonetheless often found in small companies, where communications between development, production and marketing are easy and a common objective, with strategies to implement it, can be understood by all concerned. Statistically there is evidence that a very high proportion of original inventions have come from individual inventors, without the initial backing of any organization.[1] There is a good deal of dispute about whether large or small firms are then a better environment for the development, production and marketing of a new product or process (innovation); it often depends on the scale of the R and D investment needed. Our study suggested, however, that it was easier to get a successful innovation effort going in small or relatively small enterprises. The world's first electronically controlled knitting machine has been developed by a German firm (Franz Morat) employing only 450 people. A company which challenged Tektronix successfully on oscilloscopes, by choosing the end of the market where that company was weakest, was a small British concern, Telequipment, which developed from two men and a garden shed to a company of 400 and considerable commercial success in about ten years. A small British chemical plant company has innovated some remarkably successful nitrogen plants. The Wankel rotary engine, the most radical innovation in car engine design since the beginning of the century, was turned into a viable commercial proposition by NSU,

---

[1] See J. Jewkes, D. Sawers and R. Stillerman, *The Sources of Invention*, Macmillan, 1964.

5

which 10 years ago was a motorcycle firm employing 6,000 people – a midget by the standards of the motor industry. Texas Instruments is a big company now, but 20 years ago it was a very small company which has since grown large through success.

On occasion, the systematic or accidental creation of a small unit within or attached to a larger organization can also promote an efficient innovative effort. Or a relatively small and dynamic innovative company or organization can – on occasion – act as a driving force for a much wider sector of industry or group of companies. The Marcel Dassault company, which appears to have developed a most successful variable geometry aircraft, employs only some 6,000 people – though it keeps some 30,000 employed through subcontracting. Pilkingtons used a small development team, of development and production engineers, to innovate the float-glass process.

There are good reasons for the success of small enterprises:

(1) There can be personal leadership by one or two people, whom all the other key people know, respect, and follow. Marcel Dassault, and Franz Morat (textile machinery) exemplify these qualities. In these companies there is the exciting sense of being involved in a small group working for a bold and well-conceived aim, in competition with sleepy giants.

(2) In such a small concern it is possible for a technological leader (e.g. Dassault) to guide management and broad strategy at the same time. In the same way, in the early days of Texas Instruments, three or four of their men attended the Bell symposium which unveiled the germanium transistor and, realizing its technical significance, took the investment decision to develop it fast and the commercial decision to get a small radio company to produce a first transistor radio to provide a market. Good communications and the ability to move rapidly are further inherent qualities of the small company. The production manager or a key salesman can walk into the development shop to ask a question or follow progress. Paper can be kept to a minimum.

Some of the worst as well as best companies are small ones. But Britain needs more small, fast-growing innovating concerns. In this no government can provide a substitute for the entrepreneurial spirit. But it can provide a helpful climate. Thus small companies might be systematically encouraged by government contracting (perhaps in some form akin to the Small Business legislation in the USA).

6

Before the 1965 Budget introduced capital gains tax, Britain's tax system was more favourable to capital gains and therefore to risk capital investors than the system in the USA. The 1965 Budget, however, introduced new inhibitions on growing advanced-technology companies. In addition to the new capital gains tax, legislation on close companies obliged them to distribute a proportion of their profits. The 1969 Budget relaxed the tax burden on directors of close companies. But though profits can be retained for working capital, they cannot be retained for R and D, which can be crucial in the early years. Making money is not the only, or even the key, motivation of the dynamic small business. But over-onerous tax legislation can act as a severe deterrent. Tax on R and D spending by close companies ought to be removed. Further study is needed of other possible tax incentives for small innovating enterprises, such as provision for stock options or encouragement for other forms of employee participation in capital growth.

Communications between the City sources of risk capital and the would-be entrepreneur in advanced technology are also inadequate and chancy. Though some merchant banks are beginning to take an interest, few institutional investors have staff systematically seeking out this kind of business. In the provinces, risk capital is even harder to obtain. We found that some of those in small businesses who complained of lack of risk capital had never seriously tried to get it. Too many would-be innovators lack the skills and attitude of the entrepreneur and have no idea of how to make their case to the City or what information to produce to back it up. There is room here for further enterprise in the banking community. The NRDC, too, could usefully be more imaginative in its terms. Some larger companies or groups with holdings in a smaller enterprise have been valuable sources of capital and management skill without destroying the entrepreneurial qualities of the small concern: Charles Clore and Bentley Engineering, or BATS, Imperial Tobacco and Molins are good examples. But in other cases a foster-parent has starved the smaller firm; the quality of management of the large group can be decisive here.

The Prevention of Fraud (Investments) Act, 1958 is a deterrent to the growth of small high-risk enterprises. Under it, budding private companies may not advertise for capital. They have to work through the channels of accepted City institutions which often have no expertise or interest in new and risky technologies. In the USA the American Exchange provides a recognized market in risk investments. There

7

the investor is protected, not by a prohibitive law as in this country, but by the supervision of the Securities and Exchange Commission. The abuses which inspired the Prevention of Frauds Act were real; but in today's changed circumstances the Act should be re-examined.

Above all, small concerns, like big companies, for rapid growth need access to a large market. Some (like Molins, with 70 per cent of the world market for cigarette machinery) have already managed to acquire it. But there is no doubt that, for small as well as large companies, market barriers can be a severe obstacle to optimum productivity and high output per man.

A LARGE MARKET

In many of the cases we have examined, the small size of the British market has delayed or even prevented profitable commercial exploitation of an innovation. In both capital and consumer goods the American market for new products tends to develop first, because it is richer. US companies tend therefore to be the first to acquire economies of scale and experience in production, which they then transfer to Europe.

This has been true especially of fast-moving technologies with rapid obsolescence, where the first into the market makes monopoly profits; with prices descending, the latecomers find the going harder. In one case we have examined – numerical control – a British company, Ferranti, was technologically as far ahead as American competitors in the early 1950s. Both the government and the private markets, however, developed first on a large scale in America. Now that the European market is developing, the British enterprise faces American competitors who are far better established and have already achieved big economies of scale in production.

The European market also imposes diseconomies and inefficiencies on those who serve it because it is divided, not only by tariff barriers, but also by different national standards and more varied demands. On occasion, European manufacturers therefore have to produce a wider range of products than their American rivals, and this is true of industries as varied as trucks, integrated circuits, numerical control systems and machine tools.

Nationalism has a further damaging impact, obliging the integrated circuit manufacturer, for instance, through public purchasing, to diffuse and assemble chips in several countries, thus incurring

8

extra overheads and diseconomies of scale; nuclear power stations likewise usually have to contain at least 75 per cent locally manufactured components, again limiting economies of scale.

The general strategy of seeking to widen the EEC and achieve European standards is already British government policy. But there are other useful, specific, government actions which were thrown up by the industries we studied. In electronic components, for instance, the Burghard Committee had established standards which fit in with a European standard and are becoming BS 9,000. Four major government departments at present each maintain separate inspectorates for components. The application of the new standard, followed by the amalgamation of the inspectorates, might therefore lead to big savings in manpower. The Post Office and the Defence Ministry, both massive customers, have, however, so far done little to put this decision into practice. In nuclear power likewise, where the Government has been restructuring the industry, the change ought to take a form which helps rationalization within a European market. In this key industry, Britain still has sufficient strength to be able to play a part in forming, say, two competitive European enterprises.

Our studies showed that there are industries (e.g. textile and cigarette machinery) where British and other European producers have succeeded in carving out a very large proportion of the world market, despite the many barriers and market variations described above. These barriers, however, increase costs both of marketing and of production; if he is to remain competitive with the American producer who starts from a larger domestic market, the European producer must find other means of increasing productivity or continue to have lower labour costs and hence lower living standards.

In some cases (aircraft, integrated circuits) administrative protectionism can act as a peculiarly resistant barrier; if, in such a case, high development costs are also involved, limitations on the size of the market can make it virtually impossible for a company based in a single European country to compete.

This is why action to integrate the European market for products of advanced technology is of great importance. In aviation, for instance, if the European industry remains tied to national markets and structured accordingly, it might continue to win about one-third of total home, civil business, or some £3,400 million of sales in 1980. The creation of a homogeneous market, and a reshaping of the industry to serve it, could raise the industry's turnover to some £6,800 million.

The European computer market is also growing more rapidly than the American and may be worth over £1 billion by 1975, bringing in its train an explosive growth in the market for components. Once again, growing administrative protectionism is, however, reducing the size of the market to which the individual producer has access, and lowering productivity. In these cases, as in the market for nuclear power stations and equipment, the development of common standards and the removal of administrative protectionism within Europe may have a decisive impact on the competitive standing of British and European firms.

LARGE FIRMS

While firms, large and small, can achieve higher productivity within a larger market, large-scale firms do not bring unmitigated advantages. Small firms, as we have seen, have the inherent advantage of better internal communications and less waste paper. They often provide a congenial environment for innovation; by definition they have not run to fat.

Large companies of course have other great advantages: the resources to finance large-scale development (e.g. nuclear power), automated production (e.g. vehicles) and massive marketing. But this does not infer, by any means, that large firms always exploit those advantages. There is much evidence that in Britain, in particular, a number of large companies have a very wide product range (even wider than their US rivals), operating in suboptimal conditions of production. These uneconomic operations often grow up in conditions of protection, either in the public market or through tariffs. They are often vulnerable to attack from smaller companies specializing in a particular field, especially if the attacker has access to a wider market. An example of this phenomenon is the British refrigerator industry, which has been badly hit by Italian competition. It also exists in other parts of the British electronic capital goods industry. In the motor industry, BLMH contains many suboptimal production units – inherited from its series of as yet unconsummated mergers. There are big gains to come from rationalization here.

Our studies, however, did contain at least three examples where a large firm gained major advantages from its size. One was integrated circuits, where although the Philips and Mullard companies failed in the 1950s to enter the silicon semi-conductor business, size has since then enabled them to get back into the race. A second example

10

was colour television, where RCA spent over $100 million on developing its system. Huge resources have also been necessary to finance the development of nuclear power reactors and the loss-leading which has established General Electric and Westing-house in their strong commercial position.

But bigness can also mean big mistakes, or big losses (General Electric in atomic power). As small firms grow into large ones, they lose their vital advantages of easy communications and personal leadership; the need emerges for systematic management to ensure that the communications between research and development and the market are efficient, and that there continues to be a vigorous pursuit of common goals. A good illustration of this is found in the aircraft industry. Dassault works on small-company principles, and is successful. Boeing is large, but an admirable management system gives it success too. BAC is largish too but, like many British companies, it lacks the reservoir of trained management talent that is present in the US.

This is why the merger movement in Britain could well lead to lower productivity and efficiency in some cases. Management skills are Britain's scarcest resource; yet size places much greater demands on management. Certainly it would be absurd to make size a panacea. Among the industries we studied, nuclear power, aircraft and colour television were cases where large companies showed important advantages. But there were others – like machine tools – where the largest enterprises were certainly not the most efficient, even though the minimum viable size of firm is rising in this industry.

MANAGEMENT SYSTEMS

Once a company grows large, the right management system becomes indispensable for an effective innovation strategy. The merger movement in Britain thus aggravates the acute need for better management systems and more trained managers. This is not a handbook on management, but in the companies we studied several principles emerged clearly:

(1) There must be exciting and carefully thought-out overall objectives, and strategies by which those goals are to be achieved.
(2) In execution, a good management system consists, in a sense, of creating small-firm conditions in separate divisional enterprises and profit/product centres in which marketing, production and development can be pursued as a single goal. A key factor,

11

however, must remain the disciplines and framework in which these centres operate. In Texas Instruments and one British competitor, for instance, we found apparently similar and admirably decentralized structures leading, because of different rules of the game, to dissimilar results (faster growth in Texas Instruments). In some large companies it is possible to get the worst of both worlds: limitations on 'small-company freedom' and little access to supplies of capital. Several subsidiaries of large conglomerate companies have found their development arrested by the parent's refusal to provide finance. At the same time they have been prevented from raising money outside.

(3) Movement of people, as well as information, between development and marketing, must be organized systematically.

(4) There must be a clearly defined procedure for examining the merits of innovation projects and for assessing their costs, profitability and potential. There must be a definite procedure for progressing them through the various stages of development and commercial application, with recognized milestones when a decision is made to stop, alter or accelerate a project, or simply carry on.

(5) Most important of all, the structure and the goals must be widely known and easily understood by everyone and, if possible, communications should be made in small groups through visual aids and the spoken word.

(6) Even a bad system which everyone understands and operates is better than none at all.

THE MANAGEMENT PROBLEM OF THE MATURING FIRM

A special management problem often arises when the small innovating firm crosses a whole series of thresholds as it grows in size. It may start off by developing and selling, successfully, a single product and organizing its operations by personal contact and informal leadership (e.g. Telequipment, Airmec, Morat). As its technology becomes more complex, its need for capital greater and the number of its employees more than the few hundred with whom personal contact can be maintained, its need for systematic management techniques grows.

These techniques are needed in a wide range of areas, all of them related, in one way or other, to the successful development and application of new technology. They may be needed in production, as a product like integrated circuits moves on from the early batch-production phase to mass assembly and inspection; they may be needed in marketing and customer service; they may be badly needed in industrial relations as the cement of traditional personal relationships weakens, and as systematic policies have to be followed to rationalize pay structures and to interest people systematically in their work through such things as job enrichment and deliberate participation. Above all, perhaps, they are needed in communication and in the development of clear procedures for disciplining and controlling the cost and timing of technological development.

Sometimes, as when the scale of production and worldwide marketing of a product require vastly greater resources than a small innovating firm can muster, it is appropriate for the new role to be fulfilled through the takeover by a larger firm of either a small firm or its technology. Thus a crucial issue is whether the large firm has the sensitivity to help and encourage the continuing process of innovation, or clumsily constrains it.

There are, however, many cases when so dramatic a jump in scale is not required, when a small innovating firm would grow naturally at a rapid rate, provided its management could appreciate the use for a new style of management and a new strategy and could acquire the appropriate techniques.

AN INNOVATION STRATEGY

A good management system provides the framework through which a firm can pursue an innovation strategy. This can and must contain many elements, depending on market circumstances and the economics of any particular innovation, at the time. But certain features of interest emerged from this study:

(1) Though licensing can be a useful means of catching up with the latest technology, a successful innovation policy cannot be based on licensing alone. Pilkingtons have licensed three major American companies with the float-glass process. One of the two we visited had already worked on the process; another had not. The licensing arrangement has been more successful with the company which had already done its own research. G. and E. Bradley licensed an instrument in a field where it had no previous experience; it proved difficult and very expensive to develop, produce and market a workable commercial product.

13

(2) A second, sometimes misleading, conception is that successful innovation depends automatically on fast 'lead times'. One British firm in the period 1952–56 was probably ahead of the world in the technology of numerical control systems; but until 1963 there was only a negligible European market. Other, American, companies which came in later were able to reap bigger commercial benefits and catch up. In this case the British firm in fact came in too early, and has had to sustain an excessively big development effort for small return.

(3) Fast lead times can, however, be important; indeed, in fast-moving technologies it is essential to have the scale and management skills to be able to move through the development phase quickly, if the market opens up rapidly and rivals are moving. But a major element in a successful innovation strategy is the ability to 'hover', hawklike, taking in the commercial and technological features of a market, until a moment comes to pounce. The American nuclear reactor companies and the American Atomic Energy Commission have been doing precisely this in sodium fast-breeder reactors. For some years, while Britain pushed on with development, Westinghouse and GE, like the American Atomic Energy Commission, waited, building up a capability (in components and fuel experience) and concentrating on getting a commercial return from existing BWR reactors. But in 1971, the Americans began to accelerate their fast-reactor development, sensing that the timescale for application in the market place is shortening. As so often in the aircraft and other industries, the question for Britain is whether this carefully planned, timed and fast-moving American development will once more overtake Britain's current development lead.

(4) In large companies there is a case for establishing a perhaps small strategic planning department with the task of assessing the company's wider commercial environment, strategic threats and opportunities, and inspiring the necessary executive response.

STATE INDUSTRIES

A special case of the key problem of transfer of technology from development to market is the state-owned industries and research facilities. Britain's high concentration of QSEs in R and D and science-based industries in the 1950s owed much to the pull of government demand. Now defence ambitions have been pruned, but a large infrastructure remains, employing large numbers of QSEs.

14

In the atomic energy industry the problem of transferring technology into the market place has been particularly acute; the re-organization of the industry has correctly and deliberately brought the development of reactors into the commercial organizations which market them. In the aircraft industry, development and marketing do take place in one organization. The problem is to create a genuine commercial relationship with the customer, the Government, so that the industry is impelled by valid commercial drives.

We have not visited government laboratories (other than the UKAEA), but it is plain that there is, here, an acute need to release locked-up QSE brainpower for practical ends. Research in government laboratories can be considered useful if it serves one of two purposes:

(a) supplies a definite requirement to government or public services (as does the Road Research Laboratory); or
(b) supplies scientific and technological information of economic value to industry.

Firms we contacted accepted that government research laboratories made some contribution on the level of pure and applied science and even some systems (e.g. techniques of making circuit diagrams; the mathematics of numerical control; the aerodynamic characteristics of alternative aerofoil configurations). But none has yet found that national research laboratories helped them to develop specific industrial applications. The drives, motivations and responsibilities simply are not there.

If Britain's QSEs and facilities are to be focused more clearly on economic industrial applications, there is a powerful case for concentrating in industry a larger proportion of the government funds spent on research and development. Certainly there must be a systematic effort to bring together the best areas of government R and D laboratories with the marketing, production and technical departments of the companies which can use their knowledge. One way of doing this might be for government laboratories to set up in business as research enterprises to whom industry could contract work, provided they could carry it out in a competitive way. Another way would be to allow industrial organizations to make a strictly commercial bargain with the Government for the use of a team at a government laboratory (or even of the whole laboratory) at an agreed price and for a specified term, but to allow the QSEs to remain in the scientific civil service and the laboratory to remain Government-owned in anticipation of a future government need for the facilities.

15

Some research establishments (e.g. the National Gas Turbine Establishment, whose main function is to serve one commercial company only – Rolls Royce) might be sold to industry if industry was interested in buying them; or the company and the Government might agree to share equally the total costs of the establishment, each side having equal rights of access and use of the results of work and patents. There are certainly a few government R and D establishments which have survived only for historical reasons, and some where there is confusion of function and responsibility. A major government effort, with the advice of outside consultants who have acquired the skills for such work, should be put into rationalizing this structure. Where research establishments are systematically run down, the right to transfer pensions to non-government jobs and systematic secondment into (say) teaching, could help personnel to find alternative work. In government establishments as in industry, generous redundancy arrangements going, on occasion, as far as early retirement on full pay can bring real economies in the long run. What cannot be justified economically is the preservation, for their own sake, of research establishments which do not produce economically useful results. Even the most skilled engineers are better 'drained' to America than performing interesting but uneconomic activities at public expense, at home.

The enlargement of the European Community could also be relevant to the adaptation of Britain's public-owned laboratories to wider and more economic purposes. A centre such as Harwell, for example, which as a national centre must face the prospect of a rapid rundown, might be more valuable as a source of fundamental and applied research for European industry as a whole. If such facilities were offered to the European Community as part of the common research centre, financed by the Community budget, Britain would benefit financially and the asset would be better used.

Chapter 2
POLICY ON QUALIFIED MANPOWER

THE MALDISTRIBUTION OF QSES IN BRITAIN: TOO MANY IN RESEARCH, TOO FEW IN PRODUCTION AND MARKETING

The weaknesses in production and marketing which we often found in British companies[1] are matched by the maldistribution of qualified scientists and engineers. A very large proportion (one-third) of Britain's graduate QSES is concentrated in research and development, rather than in production, marketing and other functions. This is a far larger proportion than in, say, West Germany.[2] We found striking differences, too, in the firms we studied. One small continental firm in the field of electronic components employed 70 graduates in marketing and 30 in R and D at the time of our visit. One British competitor, in the same field, employed 30 graduates in R and D and only 10 in marketing.

On the face of it, this concentration of British QSES in R and D may be imagined to produce a creditable list of inventions; and Britain's favourable balance of payments in knowhow bears this out. But it is also in part responsible for the failings in production and marketing which we have described.

THE SUPPLY OF ENGINEERS AND SCIENTISTS

What is the reason for the small numbers of graduate engineers in marketing and production in British industry?

In a study on the British economy by the Brookings Institution,[3] Merton J. Peck argues that the supply of graduate engineers and scientists has not grown fast enough and ought to be increased.

The careful study by OECD on education and the technological gap, based on comparable statistics collected as part of OECD's studies on Gaps in Technology between Member Countries,[4] conveys a

[1] See pp. 3 ff.

[2] B. R. Williams, *Technology, Investment and Growth*, Chapman and Hall, 1967.

[3] *Britain's Economic Prospects*, George Allen and Unwin for the Brookings Institution, 1968.

[4] *Differences in the Development of National Scientific and Technological Capabilities*, Analytical Report, Educational Aspect, OECD, 1968.

rather different impression. It brings out the following key points:

(1) The USA has of course a far larger *total stock* of *university graduates* in all subjects, in relation to the total labour force, than has Britain or the EEC. The figures in 1964 were: USA, 7·6 per cent; United Kingdom, 2·8 per cent; EEC, 2·8 per cent. This larger US graduate population was based on longer average schooling (10·5 years versus 8·4 years in France and 9·3 in the United Kingdom). And, of course, *output* of all kinds of *university graduates* is a far larger proportion of any given age group of 20 to 24 than in the EEC or Britain.

(2) The existing US *graduate* population incidentally includes a far larger proportion of men and women with degrees in *management and business studies*. In 1964, 63,000, or 12 per cent of the US output of graduates, had degrees in 'business and commerce' from business schools. This is far higher than the proportion in Britain, where systematic higher education in management has got under way only in the last few years.

(3) In *science and technology*, however, the disparity in the total stock of qualified scientists and engineers (i.e. graduates and equivalent professional qualifications) in relation to the size of the labour force is very much smaller. (USA, 1·62 per cent; United Kingdom, 1·05 per cent; France, 0·7 per cent; Germany, 0·65 per cent, in 1964.)

(4) If all *post-secondary higher education in science and technology* is included, the picture shows Europe and especially Britain in an even better light. In many European countries, a large proportion of higher engineering education is carried out in non-university institutions (technical colleges etc.). It is impossible to get precise figures which are strictly comparable between different countries, but it seems likely that in any age group of 20–24 the proportion which obtains some kind of higher qualification in science and technology is *highest* in the United Kingdom, closely followed by the USA, while France and Germany are somewhat further behind. In addition, Britain seems to have the largest percentage *stock* of scientists and technologists with some kind of higher qualification in relation to the size of its labour force.

(5) There is a big difference between science and engineering. Both in the USA and Britain the biggest increase in *university* graduation has been in pure science: from 27,000 to 62,500 between 1955

Table 1

Proportion of Age Group (average 20–24) Obtaining a First Degree in Scientific and Technical Subjects at University or Other Post-Secondary Equivalent, in Nine Western Countries (1964 or nearest year)

	% obtaining first degree or equivalent					
	1. Science and technology*		2. Technology†		3. Pure science	
	A	B	A	B	A	B
USA	4·2	4·2	1·48	1·48	2·39	2·39
Belgium	1·3	3·0	0·57	2·21	0·61	0·91
France	2·5	3·2	1·24	1·93	1·13	1·13
Germany	0·8	2·2	0·46	2·0	0·21	0·21
Italy	0·9	0·9	0·33	0·33	0·45	0·45
Netherlands	0·8	2·5	0·38	2·03	0·27	0·27
United Kingdom‡	2·7	5·1	1·4	2·8	1·32	1·68
Sweden	1·7	1·9	0·80	0·80	0·79	0·79
Japan	1·8	2·1	1·23	1·44	0·22	0·26

Note: Columns 1A, 2A, 3A refer to university education.
Columns 1B, 2B, 3B refer to total higher (including post-secondary non-university) education.

* Including architecture and agronomy.
† Excluding architecture and agronomy.
‡ British figures in columns A include recognized QSE qualifications such as membership of institutions; British figures in columns B include HNC and HND graduates, but an estimated deduction is made to eliminate double counting of non-university students who obtain more than one qualification.

Source: OECD Papers for Third Ministerial Meeting on Science and Technology; *Gaps in Technology between Member Countries, Analytical Report, 1968.*

and 1964 in the USA, and from under 5,000 to 8,580 in the same period in the United Kingdom, plus an additional 1,400 with equivalent higher qualifications. By 1967, over 11,000 were obtaining such graduate and equivalent qualifications in the United Kingdom.

In technology the increase in university graduation has been smaller in both countries: from 28,000 to 38,700 in the USA,

C

and from under 2,500 in Britain in 1955 to 3,723 in 1964 and over 5,000 in 1967. But in Britain over 5,000 more technologists acquire equivalent higher qualifications (membership of institutions and so forth). And if British students who pass Higher National Certificate (14,228 in 1964) are included in the British total and added to those who take first degrees, a *larger* proportion of the age group 20–24 in Britain than in the USA obtains some kind of higher qualification in technology. Including these alternative qualifications, the OECD statisticians showed that out of every 10,000 young people in the age group 20–24, 239 obtained science qualifications and 148 technology qualifications in the USA in 1964. In Britain the OECD figures were 174 for science and 308 for technology.

This series of comparisons is bedevilled by the problem of definition. Clearly the large number of British and European higher educational 'equivalents' are not the same thing as graduation through a good American university. But not all American universities are better than a British technical college. Some conclusions can in any case be drawn.

If America is taken as a model, Britain and other European countries have a long way to go to increase the total university population, lengthen schooling, increase the numbers receiving training for management, and *raise the level of training of technologists* from, say, HNC equivalent to university degrees. But, thanks to the major effort made to expand technological education in the last decade, the overall supply of engineers in Britain is astonishingly large.

Clearly, expansion of supply of graduates must go on as fast as possible. But we believe that attention must now be focused more on making better use of the qualified scientists and engineers we have, and on *increasing industry's appreciation of and demand for* qualified scientists and engineers, especially in marketing and production.

The slump in demand for graduates by British industry in 1970/71, like the slump in capital investment, reflected not declining need but inability to make an essential investment in the future.

INCREASING INDUSTRY'S DEMAND FOR QSES

In the mid-1960s, migration of qualified scientists and engineers in and out of Britain swung from a small positive net balance to a pronounced drain. In the five years 1958–62 there was a net immigration of 4,620 qualified scientists and engineers into Britain; in the following five years there was a net loss of 10,475 qualified scientists and engineers.[5] British scientists and technologists were emigrating to America because, in a decade (1956–66) which saw US annual expenditure on R and D grow from $7 billion to $22 billion, there was a more powerful demand for their services there than in this country.

The market explanation is borne out by the fact that the whole increase in net emigration has been for engineers and technologists, where the British output has increased fastest and the American least. In 1961, the emigration of British technologists was equivalent to only 24 per cent of the new supply three years earlier. By 1966 the equivalent of 42 per cent were leaving. In science, where the American supply increased more and the British less, the proportion of Britain's recent graduates to leave increased only from 22 to 23 per cent. When immigration is taken into account as well, the total net loss of qualified technologists and engineers in the years 1963–68 was 11,335, or about one year's British output of graduate and non-graduate QSEs. In science there was actually a net gain of 890.

This market explanation of demand for engineers (strong in America except in recession-time, weak in Britain) is confirmed by rates of pay. Table 2 shows how US salaries for engineers are higher than in Britain, a function of America's higher productivity. More striking is Table 3, which shows the salaries paid in 1968 by a European electronics company operating in several countries. Salaries for engineers are higher than in Britain, even in a country (like Italy) that has a lower average income per head. And when extra social security costs are taken into account, companies on the Continent pay relatively even more. The market factor is also confirmed by the differences in salary between different *branches* of engineering, shown in Table 2. Electronics and chemicals are the two best paid, for these science-based industries have the biggest demand for QSEs throughout the world. Further indirect evidence is provided by the impression we have gained that, at any rate in some companies, some British qualified engineers are not properly and fully used. In the aircraft industry there may be rather too many graduates doing routine work. We suspect that there may be other pockets of under-used engineers in the electrical industry, not to mention government laboratories.

[5] See *Persons with Qualifications in Engineering Technology and Science, 1959 to 1968*, Department of Trade and Industry, p. 31.

21

Table 2

Engineers' Salaries in the USA and UK, by Industry (1967)

(£ per year)

	Lower quartile	Median quartile	Upper quartile
All Engineers			
USA	4,562	5,208	5,950
UK	1,928	2,141	2,987
Civil			
US construction industry	4,783	5,166	5,778
UK civil engineer	1,912	2,100	2,979
Mechanical			
US machinery industry	4,186	4,791	5,283
UK mechanical engineer	1,854	2,079	2,875
Electrical			
US electrical engineering industry	4,583	5,166	5,833
UK electrical engineer	2,028	2,241	2,995
Chemical			
US chemicals industry	4,541	4,937	5,395
UK chemical engineer	2,128	2,729	3,850

Note: (a) The US salaries are for the industry of employment, while the UK salaries are by discipline.

(b) The US salaries are for an engineer of 9–11 years' experience, while the UK salaries are the average of all age groups.

Sources: UK: *The Survey of Professional Engineers 1968*, Ministry of Technology.

USA: *Professional Income of Engineers 1966–67*, Engineering Manpower Commission of Engineers Joint Commission.

Consideration of these market factors leads us to ask why demand for engineers in particular, and notably for graduates, did not grow in Britain in the early 1960s in proportion to the growth of supply. A big change is now under way. There is a growing number of companies which make vigorous and systematic efforts to recruit graduates, and have specialized staff engaged in the task of combing the universities for talent. But they are still limited in number and include few small British-owned firms.

We visited the largest British automobile and machine tool companies. Both have now instituted systematic arrangements for recruiting graduates straight from university, either centrally or in some

Table 3

A Comparison of Engineers' Pay in Five Countries: Annual Pay and Total Cost of Technicians and Engineers in a European Electronics Company (1968)

(£)

	Italy		UK		France		Germany		Sweden	
	Gross pay	Total cost	Gross pay	Total cost	Gross pay	Total cost	Gross pay	Total cost	Gross pay	Total cost
Technician:										
Starting salary	1,250	1,750	1,208	1,291	1,291	1,791	1,500	1,666	1,750	2,083
30–32 years	2,333	3,250	2,041	2,125	2,250	3,000	2,041	2,291	2,500	2,838
QSE Engineer:										
Starting salary	1,783	2,375	1,541	1,625	1,958	2,583	1,958	2,166	2,083	2,488
30–32 years	2,750	3,750	2,458	2,541	2,916	3,750	2,783	2,916	3,283	3,750
QSE Engineer:										
30–32 years, Section leader	3,666	5,000	2,828	2,916	3,958	5,000	3,333	3,750	4,375	5,000

23

divisions. Until very recently, this was, however, still on a relatively small scale. The entire British Leyland group (employing over 200,000 people) had, until 1968, been recruiting some 80 graduate scientists and engineers per year. Plans were then laid to step this up to 300 in 1969–70, though this has since been cut. By comparison, British companies in chemicals and electronics have been recruiting graduates on a larger scale for many years. But none we met matched Texas Instruments, Bedford, a firm employing 2,000 people, which in the 1960s was recruiting 20 graduates per year.

Why have the figures for the British firms been so low, especially in the mechanical engineering industries? Until the 1950s neither Leyland, nor BMC, nor Alfred Herbert, nor the main manufacturers of textile machinery, recruited graduates systematically at all, a notable contrast with the equivalent American or even German industries.

When demand for a product is uneven or weak, it is useful to find out the customer's reasons for caution. The reluctance to use and take on graduates in certain industries does not spring only from misguided conservatism. There are plainly real problems in Britain in fitting graduates usefully into industry and features of their education which could be improved. One of the most remarkable innovators in British industry remarked: 'Graduates are useless in design; they've had all their creativity educated away.' The same theme was voiced in other forms by many authoritative people. Another key innovator remarked that: 'What is taught at universities today is not engineering, but the science of engineering; engineers should be taught synthesis as well as analysis.' The theme that engineering design is an art, as well as a science, in which intuitive qualities as well as analytical powers are important, was often voiced, and the criticism made that universities do not help to awaken these qualities but can stifle them. There are of course many differences between the training of a qualified engineer in Britain and in Continental Europe. Courses on the Continent are frequently much longer. Without going into detail, we might add that a German or Italian engineering graduate's education does provide more of a training in design and industrial application.

Another favourite industrial thesis is that graduates are less well-adapted socially to industrial life than those who have become engineers via the shop floor and the traditional means of acquiring additional qualifications via night school and day release. Plainly, in caste-conscious Britain, there are problems in fitting graduates into

24

the industrial community in a way which rapidly broadens their experience and capability, and does not arouse resentment.

Finally, there is a factor to which we shall return. In the past, many people in industry have believed that graduates are suited mainly to doing academic-type research work, while chaps with Higher National Certificates and an industrial background are best suited to organize and manage production and sales. On the face of it, the view is understandable. Shop floor management is plainly done best by those with an understanding of industry. The highest mathematical capabilities may be required in R and D. But there is no doubt too that many illogical features of the British social climate widen the gulf between academics and 'practical men'.

Universities are still too often geared toward producing academic capabilities, and encourage the view, among students, that the logical conclusion of their studies is further research work. Selling machine tools is not always regarded as the highest career objective in the Groves of Academe. Not surprisingly, some people in industry reciprocate with suspicion of academically trained and all-knowing graduate engineers. Yet highly qualified people are needed as much in production and technical sales as in research, as the more progressive firms are realizing. The social attitudes which assume that a graduate's place is in the laboratory while HNCs manage the works and ONCs sell, have been a factor in the curious and uneconomic distribution of Britain's stock of QSEs.

THE ALL-ROUND MANAGER/TECHNOLOGIST

The development of the overall capability to examine market needs, develop products to meet them and get them produced and sold, according to a strategy, plainly requires QSEs in many departments other than research. Graduates can bring a systematic and scientific approach to production methods and an ability to question accepted ways, which is an indispensable element in improving productivity and the basis for a high rate of investment. In marketing, the graduate can raise the level of the operation from simple salesmanship to a means of analysing and predicting the customer's future needs and to become an integral part of the selling company's own development operations.

Other changes – some of which are already under way – will have to be carried forward more rapidly. People are needed with a wide view of technology and its economics, and an ability to think in terms of a strategy for carrying innovation through to the market place. If British industry is to be able to draw on more of such people, several changes will have to take place:

1. A change in basic national social values: many individuals still feel that they acquire greater social status by working in a government research laboratory, which may yield no immediate practical result, than by, for instance, marketing engineering products – the way in which industry discovers and serves society's needs. Somehow this has to be changed.

2. The partly valid criticisms of the engineering graduate, and indeed of the 'arts' graduate, have to be met by the educational system. Industry needs to be able to recruit people with a broad basic knowledge of technology plus an awareness of its industrial, economic and commercial application. In the past, the educational system has conceived its task to be the creation of 'professional' engineers and scientists who will remain specialists in their fields. In future, both sixth forms and universities will have to devote growing attention to educating large numbers of potential managers with an understanding of technology and its place in society.

3. Specific black spots in the educational supply of graduates need to be removed. Three have been incisively identified by Dr H. H. Gardner of BAC.[6] One of these is the poverty in Britain of systematic training and education for the job of the production engineer: that most challenging of jobs which requires knowledge of planning, advanced manufacturing techniques, production control methods, machine tools, materials and handling of labour. A second is the weakness of education for design: not the narrow skills of the drawing office, but training in that special combination of analysis, broad engineering knowledge and aesthetic and technical imagination, which leads to good design. The third of Gardner's black spots, one which may perhaps have to be remedied by training at a different level, is the absence of skilled general managers for small companies, another type of all-rounder who needs a solid technological grounding; in Dr Gardner's phrase: 'Many companies have failed completely to find a suitable trained man. They evade the problem and appoint an accountant.' One might note too the lack of awareness of the tremendous problems of management development which arise when small companies grow into large ones – problems that may require training and educational resources from outside.

[6] See Dr H. H. Gardner, *The Graduate Engineer in Industry* from Council of Engineering Institutions Conference, on the Engineers that Industry wants, 1969.

4. The problems of re-orientation from academic to industrial work are important for the scientist as well as for the engineer, but there is a greater need for a change of attitudes toward and by physicists, than chemists. Chemists in Britain are trained for six years. In the first year of university training there is no distinction between the chemist and the chemical engineer. A recognized and accepted career channel takes chemists into the chemical industry which, in 1965, employed 13,000 out of the 31,000 scientists employed in British industry. In the case of physicists, however, there is a bigger need to improve the relationship between university and industry. The education of the physicist is separate from that of the engineer from the start of his university career, and little attention has been paid to the transition from university physicist to applied engineer. Many industrial companies could make good use of physicists and not enough realize this. Too few physicists at university are industrially motivated or appreciate the potential commercial application of their studies. Thus in 1965, while 60 per cent of the nation's stock of chemists worked in industry (excluding government establishments), only 38 per cent of its physicists did so.

5. Industry itself can attract good people, if it wants them, by paying more or providing better opportunities (as firms like Ferranti and Texas Instruments have been doing), and by making university students aware of the exciting potential of industrial life. Texas Instruments, with its 2,000 employees and 20 graduates recruited each year, received 300 graduate applications for jobs in 1968. This is not because Texas Instruments pays more than comparable British companies, but because it has succeeded in conveying a glamorous image of the opportunities and potential of industrial life. The image of the Midlands, and indeed amenities in some industrial towns, may not be so attractive. But British firms also have found they can draw able young people, provided they do genuinely offer them early responsibility, a chance to develop their capabilities and exciting goals.

6. Career development, and systematic annual appraisal of staff, is being adopted in many of the firms we visited. It is important and should be properly understood, because good overall ability to carry innovation through from development to the market can come only from managers who have had experience of different aspects of the process, and whose capabilities have been systematically developed. The old-style form of training for the graduate – hang around and watch what happens – clearly does not do this.

27

Nor, indeed, is it enough merely to give the graduate a job or arbitrary 'project'. There are, however, very good ways of developing capability while carrying out a really useful function. In a good management services department, for instance, graduates can be given problems to analyse and programmes to develop which give them invaluable experience.

7. If British industrial companies are to develop effective technological strategies, more of the leaders of industry will have to have technological or scientific qualifications. The leading electrical company which we visited, none of whose board members was a graduate QSE, was hardly well-placed to pursue such a strategy. A recent survey[7] of American industry showed that half the presidents of America's 500 largest industrial companies had technical degrees in 1967. In Britain, by contrast, only 8 per cent of the directors of companies employing over 100 people were qualified engineers in 1967.[8] In too many British companies the graduate engineer has a lower status than the average businessman, reflecting the position at the top.

8. There is a need to reassess, fundamentally, the relationship of the university to industry and the place of the university in society. Industry's disquiet about the training and background of graduates is matched by the uneasiness of many graduates when they get into industry. The universities themselves rightly question their future role. There is a case for re-appraising the whole conception of the university as a place to which students go for a fixed period immediately after leaving school. Many people in industry argue that students benefit more from their studies if they first spend a period in industry. Such a period can enhance the value of studies and bridge the social gulf between graduates and those who come up via the shop floor. Sandwich courses are a useful step in the right direction; but they are still regarded by some industrial managements as a second-rate form of education, and they are excessively compressed. As the pace of technological change increases, and the need for life-long learning grows, the number of university places available to mature students ought to be drastically increased. Higher education needs to become a right for all – a source to which men or women can go to supplement their experience with new disciplines at any time in their lives.

[7] Survey by Heidrick and Struggles, Chicago, 1967.
[8] Roger Betts, 'Characteristics of British Company Directors', *Journal of Management Studies*, Vol. 4, February 1967.

9. Finally, the gap between university research and industry could be bridged more effectively if far more university research projects, including Ph.D. theses, were done in industrial workshops and laboratories, with a practical objective. When students of the Royal College of Art design delightful special toys that can be used by handicapped children, as major projects in their course, their work receives a fillip. In the same way, technical research students would get more satisfaction and stimulus from their work if it had a chance of leading to real-life developments or products, instead of to a pigeon-hole in the college library.

To work on a wide scale, such a principle requires more systematic thought by industry on what its research needs are – not the immediate, applied, development needs that will be carried out by companies, but the step ahead on which such development may be based: in the textile knitting machinery industry, for example, this might imply study of the systems which might link electronically controlled machines, of their commercial application in a seasonal consumer-oriented industry, and so on; in aerospace, it may be study of high lift devices, development of advanced wing design techniques, study of boundary layer drag, and so on. Dr Gardner's proposal is that panels be set up in each major industry and closely linked to the universities, to look at the needs of the next 10 to 20 years and orient university research to fit them. Such an approach would not only make better use of national resources, but provide an exciting motivation for university research as well. It would also fit in with the conception of an 'education spectrum': that is to say, after school a man goes into industry for a period of time, then to university where he first obtains a grounding in technology and its relation to society, and then he moves on to specialize in his particular skill. If he goes into design or research he may move through a piece of industry-oriented research before he goes back into industry.

In most of these matters, change is slowly taking place, but not fast enough.

THE COMPARATIVE IMPORTANCE OF THE MAJOR FACTORS

Is it possible to assess the comparative importance of the major factors we have described as conditioning industrial, and in particular innovative, performance? In the summaries which follow we draw conclusions on particular industries. Two perhaps stand out. In certain key industries, *size of market* was certainly of great significance in determining the lead of American companies and the difficulties Europeans have had in catching up. These were all cases of advanced technology where development costs were high, there was a major public buyer, and administrative protectionism played a part.

More generally, what we can only describe as the *market orientation* of American companies, and the close link between development and the market place which many achieved, was vital to success. To improve this, British companies require, as we have seen, not merely systematic and purposive management in the companies themselves, but a shift in the tone and balance of the educational system and in social attitudes.

Mr Harold Macmillan once described the British as the Greeks to the new Rome of America. There has been a lot of the Greek spirit in the best of British education: the interest in truth for its own sake – in 'pure' science, in engineering as a branch of mathematics. But it was not the mathematicians of the School of Athens who built the aqueducts that still provide half Rome's water supply, but the Roman engineer. In Britain, during the last hundred years, because the highest education was oriented by the Greek approach and toward producing all-round administrators of empire, all too often the leadership of industry was regarded as an inferior task and left to those tutored only by experience. So today, when we have realized that industry is the source of all our strength, and the output of graduates – of arts, science and technology – has been much increased, society is not ready to use them. The graduate in Greek philosophy is shocked to find himself fitted only for writing copy in an advertising agency. The first-class scientist produces discoveries which are developed in America, and the graduate engineer finds that the traditional management of British industry does not know how to use him, while the climate and content of his training have not suited him well to industry's real needs.

There has been too little awareness in Britain of the challenging nature of the overall management of technology: that the architects of society's future are those who lead and organize people in developing, selling and applying technology, and that this requires first, a solid grounding in technology and then, in addition, social understanding and management skills. Pericles's so-called all-round man, idealized amid the dreaming Oxbridge spires, is not a complete ideal for today's industrial society. After all, there was precious little technology – that tool of change – in the Greece of Pericles. We should look more at the Roman, Swedish or American ideal of the engineer as builder – an engineer with a wider social vision than that which a narrow specialized British education gave him in the past.

Part 2
TEN INDUSTRIES: THE CASE STUDIES

Chapter 3
VARIABLE GEOMETRY AIRCRAFT

'The crucial failure of the British system has been that no-one really knows who is responsible for what.'

Companies visited:

Boeing Aircraft Company (USA)
General Dynamics Corporation (USA)
British Aircraft Corporation (formerly Vickers) (UK)
Avions Marcel Dassault (France)
Panavia (Europe)

The development of variable geometry aircraft in the 1960s was not a happy story. BAC, though involved in the innovation from its early days, never got as far as actually developing an aircraft until the very end of the decade. Dassault built a successful variable geometry prototype, but in January 1971 the single prototype crashed. Boeing designed two aircraft, the TFX for a military requirement and a supersonic transport. Neither got beyond the paper stage. In the Western world, only General Dynamics built an operational aircraft, the F111, but by April 1970 the cost had escalated from an original estimate of $4 million per aircraft to $13·7 million per aircraft and the numbers ordered had been slashed from a peak of 2,466 aircraft to 547.[1]

Yet swing wings probably still have an important part to play on future military aircraft. Their story and the lessons from it are revealing.

THE ORIGINS

Although it is popularly supposed that the swing-wing aircraft was 'invented' by Barnes Wallis at Vickers, this is neither easy to establish nor very important in relation to later development. It seems that a number of people in Europe and America, and probably also in the USSR, realized the potential of being able to alter the aerodynamic

[1] Source: *Hearings before Sub-Committee on Appropriations for 1971*, House of Representatives, April 1970.

shape of an aircraft while in flight, probably all at the same time. During the Second World War the operational speed of aircraft rose rapidly and the turbulence and drag problems of the straight aerofoil were experienced at high speeds. In the postwar period these were partially overcome by sweeping back the wings in a fixed position, but this involved a progressively steeper angle of attack for takeoff and higher takeoff speed. Having the wings nearly straight out for takeoff and then sweeping them back for high-speed flight was a way of creating an aircraft of great versatility over a wide range of airspeeds with reasonable efficiencies.

In the UK Barnes Wallis was a notable proponent of such a design from 1946 onward, and a certain amount of work was financed at Vickers by the Ministry and the company, up to a total of something less than £5 million in the 20 years 1946–65. The team up to 1957 was about 10–20 people. In the first ten years one or two small test models were built and flown, but the degree of success they achieved is not easy to establish, because there were severe problems of remote control which meant that the aircraft's stability may not have been thoroughly evaluated. A manned VG aircraft was also started, but building was stopped about 1952.

Through a government decision, all manned supersonic flight had been stopped in 1948, at least as far as government contracts were concerned, but although the decision to stop work on the VG can be bracketed with this as a similar example of short-sighted conservatism, it seems that both the Government and the companies lacked faith in the stability of the aircraft and were not prepared to put money into solving the problems.

Meanwhile, in the USA in the late 1940s, work had been done by Bell on a piloted VG interceptor/fighter. They flew two prototypes, but also failed to solve the problem of stability, which arises from a change in the centre of pressure relative to the centre of gravity when the wing swings. Their system, of having a track for the wing to slide along, was too heavy to fly operationally.

The story should be taken up again in 1957, when Vickers sent Wallis, with Ministry of Supply backing, to visit NACA (now NASA) under the Mutual Weapons Development Programme sponsored by the USA. He took with him the results of VG work up to then, which suggests that the UK authorities felt they could do nothing more with the project and were prepared to hand it over to the USA. The Defence White Paper of 1957 forecast that no more manned aircraft would be needed in Britain for military purposes; British development work on manned aircraft was then ruthlessly cut. Very soon after this visit (and people have been tempted to say because of it) John Stack of NASA put out a paper in which he suggested that the stability problem of VG could be solved by putting the pivot outside the fuselage. This was not really given much credence by the US industry, but a small group of 20 people at Boeing, which was trying to develop some proposals for a new US strike aircraft, took in VG along with VTOL and STOL as one of the ideas to use. As a result of wind tunnel testing and some further design studies, NASA got the Department of Defence sufficiently interested to start thinking about issuing a requirement (January–December 1960). At this stage there were no other companies interested in the USA, and Vickers, although they had made a number of proposals to the Ministry of Aviation and NATO, had not had any of them accepted. It seems likely that Vickers were as far ahead as Boeing by 1959/60, but they had no success in interesting the military authorities. The British were preoccupied with mergers and TSR2.

In December 1960–January 1961 the US Secretary of Defence, Gates, was replaced by McNamara. By March 1961 the concept of commonalty had been introduced into Defence Department (DOD) projects. In other words, to produce economies of scale, future aircraft should be adaptable to as many different military needs as possible. The new approach held up the issue of a Request for Proposal (RFP) on the TFX (which later became the F111), and caused a work statement to be put out instead, which alerted Boeing's competition. After a rather protracted series of further design studies, General Dynamics was awarded the contract, on the basis of a higher commonalty (72 per cent) than Boeing (60 per cent) and, apparently, on a conviction that Boeing had under-priced. The actual commonalty achieved is about 60 per cent.

General Dynamics came into the story between the end of 1960 and the beginning of 1961, when they were conducting design studies to the DOD work statement. They have asked us not to reveal what scale their manpower effort was on the development and production of the F111, but the total cost of R and D and technical work was $1,875 million by April 1970[2] and we have information available from both BAC and Dassault about their teams.

Dassault became interested in VG toward the end of 1962 when they were looking round for a new strike aircraft to sell to the French

[2] Sub-Committee on Appropriations, *op. cit.*

Government and to export. They were studying vertical lift, but realized that the speed of getting VTOL into service would depend on the development of engines, which would probably mean, for the performance they required, that the aircraft would not be in service until the mid-1970s or later.

Characteristically, Dassault wanted the plane in service fast and so turned to variable geometry where they could rely on themselves. This was soon after Jacques Alberto of Dassault had visited Boeing, after the TFX proposal had been submitted – but he had gone essentially to discuss vertical takeoff, for Boeing had been interested in Dassault's experience with the Balzac and Mirage. Alberto spent some time at Boeing in 1963 when getting the Dassault Falcon certified, but there is no reason to suppose, on either occasion, that he got any more information about VG than a general feel for the unprofitable lines of development and a certain amount of transmitted enthusiasm.

Dassault's concept of and decision on variable geometry aircraft were their own. Dassault did some design studies in 1963 and put a proposal to the French Navy in 1964 for a twin-engined aircraft, which would in their view have been a better aircraft than Mirage G, but it is said that Rolls Royce or the British Government refused to go into production with the RB153 engine. This was the one small engine available and which Dassault much liked. They believe that if this aircraft had gone ahead it would be sweeping the F104 replacement market today.

Dassault had to fall back on a single-engined aircraft and so turned to the SNECMA Pratt & Whitney 306. Then Dassault went ahead with the G on a prototype basis, and after design studies in 1964/65 (with a team of 40 people) they built the prototype in the two years from November 1965 to first flight in November 1967. The French Government financed this at a cost of about £10 million but Dassault spent approximately £1 million on the various stages.

BAC have never really dropped out of the VG business. Apart from the proposals (1959–64) made for various aircraft, part of Wallis's team went to Preston in 1965 to help start up the work on the proposed Anglo-French variable geometry aircraft for which the Warton factory was the British partner. Warton had already done some work on an aircraft called the P45 which would have been VG. Their work with the French started very soon after Dassault had begun design studies on the Mirage G. But whereas the G was built to a general understanding between Dassault and the French

38

Government as quickly as possible without any detailed control, the AFVG was the subject of constant detailed consultations between Dassault and BAC, BAC and the Ministry of Aviation, and Dassault and the French Ministère des Armées. In the two years it took to build the G, the AFVG only progressed through two or three specification changes and got bogged down in a quibble over design leadership. As Dassault's chief engineer puts it, 'the old man gave us *carte blanche* at the beginning and we quickly agreed with BAC on a 16-ton plane. But then the specification went up and down like a yo-yo, with endless committees involved. Dassault hated them and he decided he'd had enough.'

Immediately after the French withdrawal, BAC had about 175 QSES, and about 25 of lower technical standing, on the VG project. Dassault had 150 QSES on the G prototype at the peak period of development. General Dynamics used a very much larger number of people at both the design study and development stages, but they were building a substantially more complex aircraft and were using development batch methods.

There will probably be a great deal more to say about VG in ten years' time; the F111 of General Dynamics failed to achieve target performance and for some time was subject to engineering 'bugs' (e.g. stress failure due to hairline cracks in the wing pivot). The US navy cancelled its order because the aircraft failed to meet its requirements; the price has escalated. The VG SST design by Boeing was dropped by the company and replaced by a fixed-wing project, which was cancelled too. The Dassault G prototype crashed in January 1971, though a twin-engined operational prototype is now flying.

AN APPRAISAL OF THE CONTRIBUTION OF EACH
COMPANY

BAC/Vickers have 20 years' experience of VG, but apart from the aircraft which was discontinued in 1952 they have not yet started to cut metal on a full-scale flying version. By 1959 they knew how to do the technology[3] and the company could take at least some share, or maybe half, of the credit for inventing the system. This would depend on whether John Stack or Vickers first conceived the design which allowed Boeing to go ahead. For at least 10 years out of the 20, BAC were looking for a 'perfect' solution; during the remainder of the period they were trying to fit the aircraft types which they thought

---

[3] Although it seems that Wallis may not have appreciated the significance of the pivot position outside the wing until after his visit to NACA.

could be developed into the requirements generated by the services, but were unsuccessful.

Boeing is an outstandingly successful company in aircraft manufacture, but even so it has been unable so far to make any more out of VG than BAC. It had two paper aeroplanes: the TFX proposal rejected in 1962 and the swing-wing SST. For the TFX it is plain that the economy and flexibility of the concept may only be attainable after a great deal of modification. For the SST it seems that range and payload did not fit into a satisfactory equation for reducing seat-mile costs. But even though its TFX was never built, Boeing performed the achievement of taking the concept from the theoretical to the practical engineering stage. Further than that, Boeing was also instrumental in persuading the US military authorities that such an aircraft was possible and useful.

General Dynamics is the most difficult company to assess since the answers to all the interesting questions lie in the 'security' area. Most important, we cannot tell whether they developed an independent technology for VG or whether they received indirect transfer from Boeing through the Department of Defence. Tentatively we would say that the contribution of GD was not of great importance to the technology.

Dassault cannot be called a real contributor nor an innovator to the VG technology, but it seems possible that it has built the best version to date employing that technology. It has plainly built a successful wing joint, the crux of the design (GD's is said to be too big, one reason for the aircraft's instability), and claims that the G prototype (with a performance of Mach. 2·4 and 100 knots landing speed) was one of the most trouble-free the company has had. Its primary success, in this as in other aircraft, was in making use of a technology demonstrated by other companies, to produce the aircraft that makes almost the maximum use of the technology's advantages. Even so, the company was prevented from building the aircraft which it thought would be the optimum solution (the French naval aircraft proposal in 1964). By early 1971 no production orders for the Mirage G had been placed, so it was not yet a commercial success, and the loss of the prototype set back development. The French Government, however, has placed a development contract for a twin-engined version (the G8); the first prototype flew in May 1971; the aircraft should become operational about 1976.

Dassault believed for some time that a Spey-engined G would be a quick way of producing a single-engined European VG to fill

40

the gaps in the market. They would then have been prepared to start work with BAC on developing a twin-engined version, but only if the companies – not committees – led the design initiative. in accordance with Dassault's philosophy.

Table 4
Development Teams in Four Aircraft Firms (1967/68)

Company	Total employment (1)	Development department (2)	Development QSE (3)	(3) as % of (2) (4)
Boeing	147,000	28,000	15,000	54
General Dynamics (Fort Worth division)	27,000	3,800	2,500	65
BAC	36,000	6,000	1,650	28
Dassault	6,000	800	305	38

CONTRASTS BETWEEN THE COMPANIES

Total employment at Dassault in 1967/8 was approximately 4 per cent of that at Boeing, and was less than a quarter of Boeing's development department alone. Dassault's development department was only 3·5 per cent of Boeing's in total staff, and employed only 2 per cent of the number of QSEs at Boeing. How is it that Dassault has been able to build a VG aircraft, a project requiring about five times the effort at General Dynamics? How does Dassault succeed at all in the aircraft industry?

The explanation is partly to be found in the organization of the Dassault company. Although the development department is only 800 people, the whole company is more like the development group of a large company than an organization with the full range of production activities. On most of its aircraft Dassault subcontracts large parts of even the airframe production so that some 30,000 people outside the company are kept employed at the peak period of a contract.

AIRCRAFT DEVELOPMENT
The Dassault Way

Further explanation is provided by the way in which Dassault develops the aircraft before the production phase. The company believes in the development philosophy of building one prototype

41

without a detailed specification, leaving its options open on equipment and design refinements. Then the aircraft is put through a fairly long period of air and ground tests, during which the technical specifications become closely defined. The French procurement authorities, the Ministère des Armées, have favoured this system because it gives the Government the chance to compare competing aeroplanes at a stage when a very practical comparison can be made and yet very little money has actually been spent. The disadvantages are that prototype testing does take a very long time, and if one prototype is lost through a crash, the programme is put back nearly to its starting point. But it is a good method of building aircraft which contain advanced concepts; less risk of expensive failure is involved, and up to the 1950s it was in fairly general use throughout the world as the standard method. An additional advantage is that the financing of a project is easier to arrange on this basis. The Ministère des Armées can place a cost-plus contract for the relatively simple prototype and keep the total budget within reasonable limits without having to cramp the company's freedom to make technical and cost decisions by detailed control; it may then extend the contract through various phases of testing without being committed too far ahead. The effect on the industry is to create an atmosphere of considerable uncertainty about future work, which can be bad unless the companies are prepared at certain stages to back their own ideas and put in risk capital of their own – which Dassault is prepared to do (e.g. with the Mirage III, developed from the Mirage I). For a project for which there is a clear requirement, prototypes may be built on a fixed-price basis, with an agreement that modifications required by the Government be paid for by it and those due to the company be paid for by the company.

One should add that this relatively simple method of getting aircraft through the development phase makes possible huge economies in manpower on the government side. Whereas the British system of supervising detailed costs (often on a cost-plus basis) means employing several hundred people in the Technical Costs Department of the Ministry of Aviation, the French department consisted of only 30 people in the late 1960s. When fixed-price contracts are placed in France, relatively rough-and-ready yardsticks (i.e. an estimate of manpower costs and needs) are used, plus haggling. But there is no doubt of the economies in administration. Finally, decisions to back an aircraft are taken by a small number of technically competent, high-level people with whom men like Dassault have a close relationship of mutual respect, not by non-technical administrators in a large bureaucracy.

In America the main system of procurement for the last ten years at least has been to have very formal, clearly defined procedures of development, based upon a *batch* of development prototypes. The object of this is to shorten lead times at the testing stage by carrying out different testing phases concurrently on a number of aircraft built close to final specification. This requires that the technical specification of the aircraft is very clearly defined before any metal is cut. There is initially a design study phase, during which the services issue a Request for Proposal (RFP). The proposal emerging from the company is subject to a prolonged project definition phase, aimed at producing a technical specification which may run to 20 volumes of description and forms the basis of the contract agreed between the company and the Department of Defence. Boeing's workforce on the contract definition stage of the TFX proposal reached a peak of about 400 technical personnel. The development batch method requires a very heavy input of professional skills for detailed planning, and it is very expensive if anything goes wrong. By comparison, the Dassault VG prototype was really only using a maximum of 150 people at the building stage.

It is not only the development philosophy which marks out Dassault as different from other aircraft manufacturers in Europe. The company would best be described as autocratic were it not for the unusual role of the supposed autocrat – M. Dassault. Company structure follows classical lines of a managing director having the main departments – administration, technical, exports, production – under him with line responsibility to him and a staff relationship to each other. But Vallière is managing director, not Dassault, who does not appear on the organization chart. His position is described by employees as that of a technical adviser, which means that he is the creative, driving force and the key figure in decision-making. The company disappeared during the war when Dassault was detained by the Nazis, and it has thus faced a tremendous challenge in building up since the war. Until 1967 it had kept out of all merger moves, almost as if from a desire to stay in 'fighting trim'. Before the war the key engineers used to work on Sunday morning as a regular practice. Now they are sufficiently relaxed to stop on Saturday afternoon (5.00 p.m.).

Older members of the company share in profit-sharing up to a quarter of salary. This helps to compensate for the salaries which,

43

although good at the 30-year-old level (£3,000), are not high for 50-year-old men (£4,500). The company personnel see themselves as working personally for M. Dassault, and the atmosphere of loyalty and cohesion is strong enough to be a positive asset.

On the other hand, there is little suggestion of management systems about the company's working, which is in keeping with development policy. Their policy on R and D and sales is basically a version of the 'small business technique'. M. Dassault and a few other collaborators assess the coming needs of Government without recourse to any marketing department. Saturdays are used for top-level management discussions of problems, plans and achievements, but there is no background of budgetary or project control by paper-work. The aircraft Dassault builds have not been worked up by slavish attention to a government specification but are the ones the company feels to be right. This characteristic is held in common with Boeing – the determination to show the Government what it really wants and not merely to build what it has asked for – although Boeing formalizes the procedure which decides this. In seeking export deals Dassault's key men are often those who have recently been on the development team of the aircraft. The managing director, Vallière, negotiated the sale of Mirage III to Belgium. The export technical director who, with one assistant, negotiated the Australian and Swiss sales of Mirage III was head of the development team which designed Etendard. The objective of all Dassault's aircraft projects is not to achieve the latest in advanced concepts, but to utilize existing technology and components where possible with a strict eye on what characteristics could be promised to a customer and definitely and rapidly achieved at a competitive price. The case of the Mirage III, for instance, of which Dassault has sold over 1,000 throughout the world, illustrates the company's philosophy.

After the Korean War, the Americans told the French of the lightness and climb capability of the MIGs. The French Government therefore decided to sponsor a twin-engined Delta interceptor, which would be lightened by having no electronics. It would have a sharp nose and would be vector-guided from ground-based electronics. Three prototypes were ordered by the Government: the Trident, the Durandel and the Mirage I.

Dassault decided that ground electronics would be too vulnerable and so conceived a new version, with enlarged nose containing the electronics and a single, larger (Atar) motor. They asked the French Government: can we use the wings and some parts of Mirage I?

The French Government agreed and Dassault, with his own money, built the first successful prototype which reached Mach 1·7. The French Government then ordered ten pre-production aircraft. Meanwhile, Trident and Durandel crashed and so the Mirage III became the established winner.

The company does not want to be made dependent on government patronage by developing vastly expensive devices of which costs and performance are unknown. This only makes you ready for the axe when government policy changes, in Dassault's view.

In short, Dassault is a company which wants to live in a competitive environment where the company itself maintains overall control over technical decisions and costs and is not dependent on continuing government favours to survive. It seeks a commercial relationship between customer and supplier, rather than a dependent one.

The American Way

The American companies we visited expressed great admiration for the Dassault way of life, in spite of the fact that their own operating conditions are very different. Boeing and General Dynamics are both very large companies; the former is devoted entirely to aerospace, the latter is part of a conglomerate group. Their size makes it necessary that the formalized procedures on government contracting be mirrored by formalized procedures on every aspect of company activity.

Both companies have elaborate personal development systems, based on assessment of the employee by his superiors and himself. The mention of project selection is a signal for the production of organization charts, project assessment forms and questionnaires, literature on project scoring systems and timetables showing the stages of R and D programmes. This approach to project selection and development programmes is sometimes characterized by European companies as the American habit of steam-rollering problems. In fact, having a QSE ratio of 50 per cent in the development area may be the only effective way of planning to avoid problems at the testing or production stage if the batch method of developing highly complex prototypes is used.

The relationship of the American companies with the Department of Defence (DOD) is not of the same straightforward commercial nature as in France. There is a recognition that the two sides are more heavily committed to each other because of the development system employed. Informal contacts exist, and usually take place at all

45

stages of a contract, but basically the companies and the DOD work toward a formalized contractual relationship, in which the ground rules of the conduct of a programme are closely defined so that each side has a clear idea of its responsibilities in the task.

No-one can say that the history of the F111 contract vindicates the American method of aircraft development. The cost escalation of each aircraft (the cost in April 1970 being some three and a half times the original contract price) comfortably exceeds the two- to threefold escalation which hindsight has shown to be historically common. The aircraft failed to achieve the degree of commonalty expected for it and in consequence the naval order was cancelled.

No contractual system, however, is proof against wobbling objectives and the attempt to pile too many diverse and novel technical features on to one aircraft. This is what happened to the F111, partly because of the deliberate attempt to make one aircraft fulfil many needs. The TFX requirement was first drafted in 1958; at that stage the purpose was to develop a low-level interdiction aircraft for use in Central Europe (the same requirement as TSR2). In 1961 the commonalty requirement was introduced, which meant adapting the aircraft to fly from naval aircraft carriers and operate at higher altitudes. In 1965 replacement of the B52 bomber was thrown in as well. In 1963 a new sophisticated avionics requirement was added for the Mark II version (to facilitate low-level flight as with TSR2).

The sophisticated avionics, however, tended to make the aircraft too heavy for naval carrier operation, so great efforts had to be made to lighten the aircraft; these included the use of a lighter and therefore less robust wing joint. The first production aircraft then developed stress failures in the wing joint, so special stronger titanium joints were developed. In all, seven different versions of the aircraft were developed; as only 547 were ultimately produced (instead of the 2,466 at one time planned), unit costs were absurdly high. After all this chopping and changing the first operational wing of the aircraft was expected to come into service in January 1971 (instead of June 1967). As General Glasser, head of the programme, admitted to a congressional committee in April 1970: 'Many of the difficulties . . . have been those that derive from trying to do too many things with the same basic airplane. Had the airplane had a less extensive set of specifications, it might have been a lot more successful in its development,' or in the words of Congressman Ferguson: 'Did you ever hear the old adage: Too many cooks will spoil the pie?' General Glasser:

46

'That is exactly what has happened to this program: too many people pushing and pulling.'

The truth is that by the early 1960s aircraft procurement, on both sides of the Atlantic, was running into grave difficulties as technology continued to get more complicated and expensive but the bulk of funds were channelled into the missile race. With funds limited, defence authorities therefore tried to develop aircraft which would be both very advanced and multi-purpose. With only Britain's small resources behind it, the TSR2 collapsed under the weight of this endeavour and was fortunately cancelled. The F111 went ahead, but at great cost.

Its lack of success is a judgement, not on the swing-wing principle nor on the American conception of negotiating a detailed, formalized, contractual relationship between purchaser and supplier, but on the abuse to which this system was subjected; in this case the system was asked to carry a major innovation in technology and a great variety of changing military requirements all at the same time. In our view when a wholly new technology is being developed there is much to be said for first developing a single prototype, as Dassault did, as a tool for learning. Batch development is suited for aircraft that are within the state of the art, but clear objectives are needed if the aircraft is to be developed successfully. With the F15 the American authorities have now very consciously reverted to the development of an aircraft with a narrow, specific aim, though even here costs are escalating.

The British Way

In Britain there has been an unfortunate tendency to fall between the two philosophies and to get the worst of both worlds on many occasions. The industry was upset by major structural changes almost every year from 1957 to 1967 and, like the American, has had to cope with frequent changes in procurement policy. It took many years for BAC to digest fully the effects of its creation by the merger of Vickers, English Electric (Aircraft) and Bristol in 1959.

The history of VG in Britain up to 1957 illustrates the sort of pride in technical advance which leads to projects' being cancelled or abandoned because something too clever is being attempted needlessly. Wallis wanted to build an aircraft with no stabilizer (tail), and in trying to do so he failed to make use of the solution he had developed, consciously or unconsciously, to the stability problem in VG aircraft. This is the opposite of Dassault's determination to build what will work.

47

After Wallis's visit to the USA and the work done on a joint programme at NACA, Vickers – or BAC as it was soon to become – should have been in possession of enough information to carry out a successful project on a VG aircraft. But although quite a number of proposals were made, to GOR339 (TSR2) in 1959, to NATO BMR3 and CR356 in 1962, and for the P45 and P46 from the Warton (formerly English Electric) division in 1964/65, none of these were fully acceptable to the services. The obvious alternative was for BAC to go ahead on a limited scale independently – perhaps by developing a single prototype after the Dassault method. This was not done because the company had burnt its fingers badly on the Vanguard and the VC10. Further development capital was not forthcoming from the shareholders.

In the early 1960s, major decisions of this kind were evidently complicated by the problems of a newly merged company. For some time the major divisions of BAC continued to operate as virtually independent enterprises. Company decisions were taken through regular meetings of the BAC (operating) executive board at which the divisional heads put forward their suggestions as and when appropriate, and a committee-type decision was taken on whether or not to adopt them.

Junior personnel on the technical side may not have always had the chance to get their views heard because they were not present. The clearly defined procedures and vigorous comparative economic and technical analysis of competing projects found in US companies was not so characteristic of BAC at that stage. Only four out of ten board members had technical qualifications of degree standard.

In recent years, however, there has been a notable improvement in procedures for selecting and controlling major projects. Sir George Edwards, managing director of the company, takes personal responsibility for this. He is serviced by a key executive, formerly chief engineer of the Weybridge division, whose job it is: to ensure a full and detailed flow of technical information up from the divisions, to organize and present this systematically, and to service and guide the recommendations of the technical committee, which consists of the managing directors of the divisions. A larger proportion of the board have technical qualifications. And BAC's efforts to develop new projects are fed by a closer study of market requirements. Whatever one's views on the virtues of the project, the marketing effort on the BAC311, for instance, was impressive.

A significant hindrance to BAC's efforts to modernize itself is still the shortage of certain types of key manpower: mechanical and

48

production engineers; aeronautical engineers who are also trained in management; technicians and draughtsmen of the HNC type – at least until the further progress of computerization cuts down this latter need. But, as in other British companies we visited, a change to more systematic management development and management of development is under way.

Overshadowing the whole picture of military aircraft contracts in Britain is a failing in the procurement system which is in marked contrast to the American or French situation. The predominant type of arrangement for military development since the mid-1950s has been an unhappy mixture of the development batch and the single prototype systems. It is like the batch system in that a number of aircraft are built for development testing, but the contract does not make detailed technical specifications the basis of the industry's work. Only an Operational Requirement is issued. The drawing up of the Requirement has been tightened and made the subject of more lengthy feasibility and design studies before cutting metal, particularly since the Gibb–Zuckerman Report of 1961. But because there is not a group of volumes specifying in detail how the tasks are to be tackled and what the penalties are, for both Government and industry, of not sticking to the contract, the fulfilment of the Requirement encourages the loading up of the project with many advanced concepts, necessary and unnecessary, by the company and the defence research establishments. This is what happened with TSR2. Costs escalated and time went by to the point where cancellation was almost inevitable. This philosophy, of leaving design options open and adopting a strategy of making choices in the short run, is one that can work on the single prototype method but is too expensive on a batch of aircraft. The relationship between the customer and the supplier is neither a straight commercial nor even an openly dependent one. *The crucial failure of the British system has been that no-one really knows who is responsible for what.* The contract for a development batch does not specify precisely what the company is to do or how it is to do it; nor does it prevent irresponsibility on the part of the Government – adding refinements, changing requirements and extending the timetable.

SOME RECOMMENDATIONS FOR DEVELOPMENT CONTRACTS

All this has morals for government development contracts which deserve to be spelt out. In the first two chapters of this study we have drawn general lessons from the case studies as a group. To overcome the specific weaknesses in aircraft procurement which we have described, we recommend:

(1) That batch development is used only for aircraft which are within the state of the art.
(2) That clear financial penalties are arranged: on the contractor if he is responsible for raising costs above those agreed at the time of the contract; on the customer if he changes the requirement or specification.
(3) That single prototype development is used for any aircraft in which it is proposed to use or develop technology beyond that currently practised. Such aircraft may or may not be a basis of prototype competition.
(4) That the basis of contract be a performance requirement.
(5) That the prototype be paid for on a cost-plus basis, when the technology is a major advance on current practice.
(6) That the prototype be paid for on a fixed-price plus incentive contract when the technology is a minor advance on current practice.
(7) That the customer may specify what level of technical solution will satisfy his requirement on the cost-plus contract, after the contract has started and when he is given estimates of alternative costs.
(8) That this negotiation be conducted by the customer with technical costs experts as advisers only.
(9) That the contractor be given full design and cost responsibility for the fixed-price type of contract.
(10) That cost control in the case of cost-plus contracts be limited to an accountant's assessment of chargeable costs and in a fixed-price contract to an accountant's estimate of incentive earnings.

It also seems that there is a need to persuade aircraft companies to spend their own funds on developing aircraft for military applications. This is desirable because the procurement and service authorities do not always foresee correctly their real needs; changes in foreign and defence policy can give rise to an unexpected requirement in the short term. Marcel Dassault has repeatedly fixed the pattern of French government buying, by exploring the requirement and then backing a design with his own money until it is sufficiently successful to get government support.

Further Recommendation

Comparable initiatives by British companies might be achieved by announcing that a sum of 10 per cent of the aircraft procurement budget will be reserved every year for unplanned expenditure. This sum would be used only in the event of an unforeseen requirement's arising which demands 'off-the-shelf' purchase of equipment, fills the requirement and is in a sufficient state of readiness. This sum could be used for purchasing a small number of aircraft or for purchasing a proven development model at a commercially agreed price, not at cost price. If unspent, the reserve might be carried over to the next year or else placed in the planned budget for the following year, and a new reserve started. These general trends in procurement would bring the British system rather closer to the French.

LESSONS FOR EUROPE

Are there any lessons to be learnt from our examination for attempts to develop a VG aircraft as a European operation? In the case of the Anglo-French variable geometry aircraft, there was, of course, great difficulty in even establishing a requirement. Development would have been by the *batch development method*, with cost escalating in consequence of the wobbling requirements. Dassault and BAC agreed, relatively easily at first, on a common specification. But the vicissitudes of the requirement, and Dassault's dislike of committees and blurred responsibility, soon prompted him to encourage the French Government to break the project off.

THE MRCA

The British, German and Italian Governments have since agreed to develop jointly a multi-role combat aircraft (the Panther) to replace the Lockheed F104 as Italy's and Germany's main interceptor aircraft and perform the strike/interdiction/recce role once envisaged for the TSR2 and F111. The experience of the abortive Anglo-French VG aircraft, and of many other previous joint and national projects, suggested three morals for this proposed new venture, in addition to the ten listed above:

(1) The Governments should first *establish a clear requirement* if cost escalation is to be avoided and the responsibilities of both customer and manufacturer are to be clearly defined.
(2) The Governments should *give clear design responsibility either to*

E

51

one company with the others as commercial subcontractors or to a totally integrated joint development team.

(3) Since the aircraft involves an important advance in the state of the art, *the best form of contract* is that used by Dassault – i.e. *a single prototype.* The risks of batch development for a VG aircraft have been abundantly demonstrated by General Dynamics' F111.

Despite the loss of Dassault's first prototype we believe that the risks of developing this technology by the batch method are great. If the Dassault company, which has already flown a prototype, were a member, the partners would be ready to move on to development of pre-production aircraft armed with the vital knowledge on the aerodynamics of variable geometry which can only come from flying an aircraft.

What has happened in practice in the MRCA? Consideration (2) (a joint development team) is being fulfilled through the establishment of Panavia, a joint company between BAC, Messerschmidt-Bolkow Blöhm and Fiat, which will develop, produce and market the MRCA, and Turbo Union which brings together Rolls Royce, Fiat and MTU in the RB199 engine. In the project definition phase MBB held 50 per cent of the shares, BAC 33 per cent and Fiat 17 per cent. In the present, more important, development phase the balance has shifted to 42·5 per cent each for BAC and MBB and 15 per cent for Fiat. Turbo Union is owned 40 per cent by Rolls Royce, 40 per cent by MTU and 20 per cent by Fiat. Clearly the degree of integration of the development programme is not so great in such a joint subsidiary as in a single company, but the joint engineering effort seems to be going well. The managing director of Panavia (who comes from MBB) might be supposed in theory to be the arbiter, if his systems engineers cannot reach agreement on some crucial feature of the design – say the wing joint. In practice, as Dr Langfelder, the German director of systems engineering in the project, put it: 'if Mr Heath [the British director of systems engineering] and I cannot reach agreement there will be no project.' The spirit of equality on which MRCA is based condemns the partners to agree.

Within the overall framework of Panavia, the detailed development of different parts of the MRCA is shared out between the companies. At one stage there were differences over who does what but they eventually settled themselves. The centre fuselage, involving the crucial wing joint, and over a third of the work, went to MBB which at that stage (the contract definition phase) was the only member of the group that expected to do more than 33 per cent of the work. BAC is to do the nose and tail, including the flying controls and the important engine mounting (apt for a Rolls Royce neighbour). Fiat gets the wings. On the basis of this division of labour, co-ordinated and planned by Panavia, the companies seem to have developed an effective working partnership, which marks an important step forward from earlier joint projects in which the partner companies were less intimately linked.

Consideration (1), however (fixing a clear requirement), has been much less satisfactorily fulfilled. The British, German and Italian needs diverged from the start because the three airforces have different operational requirements, which caused the three Governments to plan at first for the costly development of two variations of the aircraft: a two-seater for Britain and a single-seater for Germany and Italy. Costs were cut by the German decision, in 1970, to order the two-seater version after all, but in consequence the German order was reduced in size (more US Phantoms have been bought) and Italy was left in a difficult position. The different missions, dictated in part by geographical position, mean constant pressure, however, for different equipment for the aircraft, a pressure which all concerned in the project have somehow to resist if costs are not to escalate.

As for (3) (adopting the single-prototype method of development), ten prototypes are in fact being built, adapted to the needs of the different airforces. The decision to plump for batch development is historically understandable. The three Governments need the aircraft urgently for their practical purposes, without the delay which they feel would follow from first building an aerodynamic prototype. But cost and perhaps the quality of the aircraft may suffer in consequence.

An important advance in the *management structure* of the common procurement arrangements will at least help to contain the centrifugal pressures. Matching the common companies, Panavia and Turbo Union, which are developing the aircraft, the Governments have set up a common procurement agency, NAMMA, to supervise development of the aircraft. It lives in the same Munich building as Panavia.

Since batch development is being used for an aircraft involving much new technology, it is, however, going to be difficult to negotiate a contract which places responsibility and financial penalties for cost escalation firmly on the contractor's shoulders when he is at fault, and on the customers' when they are (see (2) to (10) above). The design is evolving too much *en route*. Indeed, the very competence

53

Chart A
Panavia: Organization Chart

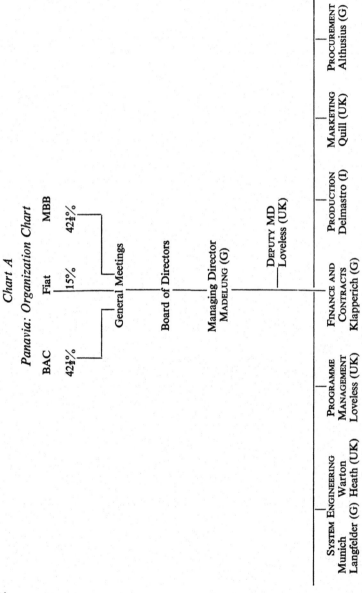

BAC	Fiat	MBB
42½%	15%	42½%

General Meetings

Board of Directors

Managing Director
MADELUNG (G)

DEPUTY MD
Loveless (UK)

SYSTEM ENGINEERING	PROGRAMME MANAGEMENT	FINANCE AND CONTRACTS	PRODUCTION	MARKETING	PROCUREMENT
Munich Langfelder (G) Warton Heath (UK)	Loveless (UK)	Klapperich (G)	Delmastro (I)	Quill (UK)	Althusius (G)

54

of NAMMA, plus engrained habit in Whitehall and inexperience in Germany, threaten to cause too much detailed intervention by the purchasers in the MRCA programme, leading in turn to divided responsibility and escalating costs. All subcontracts by Panavia worth over 100,000 DM have to be approved by NAMMA. Indeed, Panavia staff complain that they spend more time preparing reports for NAMMA than in getting on with planning and developing the aircraft. Both in Britain's aviation procurement departments and in NAMMA itself, there are a large number of excellent control staff who on occasion feel they know better than the companies developing an aircraft. The trouble is that the long-term interest of the project would be better served if the supervisors stepped back and placed responsibility firmly on the shoulders of the contractors.

There is a danger too that development costs may escalate as the German industry, short of development work, seeks to finance its R and D via the MRCA, as the British industry did with the TSR2. An overload of passengers could sink the ship.

Confronted with M. Dassault's claim that he can develop an operational VG aircraft for £40 million compared with the £240 million estimated for the MRCA, those responsible for the MRCA claim that Marcel Dassault's £12 million prototype was a non-operational aircraft without equipment and that it will cost much more to make it operational. It is not a fully convincing explanation of the discrepancy.

Dassault himself waits on the sidelines and in 1968–70 (i.e. throughout the period of this study) declared himself willing to embark on a joint venture with the British provided the companies settle the design.

The truth is that the European industry badly needs more of the Dassault style in the management of development. Yet, those who have been trying to develop a European aircraft industry, in recognition of the facts of large scale, are right too.

Dassault has ended up with an excellent prototype without a market. Even if the military version of his variable geometry aircraft goes ahead, it will be excluded from the vital German, British and Italian markets.

FUTURE TASKS

What can be done to rectify this wasteful and unfortunate situation? It is certainly absurd that after a decade of effort to bring the aircraft programmes of Europe together, the most expensive, advanced

55

and important military requirement of the major European states should be satisfied by duplicate developments – a potential separation which could last till the end of the century.

The specific need is somehow to graft together the Dassault and Panavia development efforts. It could probably only happen when later versions of the aircraft are developed. Such a combination would be clinched if the three key partners – MBB, BAC Warton and Dassault – could move on from the present, specific, co-operative projects which link them together to a full-blooded merger.

Such a step has to be matched by movement on the government side as well. Here there seem to be three issues. First there will almost certainly be no coming together of the MRCA and Dassault programmes without a considerable effort at government level and a real political determination to develop common defence requirements. Second, this is not just a matter for the French and British. Bonn has to resist constant massive pressure from the Americans to buy aircraft in the USA and will not do so unless West Germany acquires a stake in development and technology. Nor will such an understanding prove durable unless it is translated into some practical institutional form such as a common defence procurement agency – which could be a development of NAMMA, in the same way as a European military aircraft company could build on the experience and substance of Panavia.

Third, and of vital importance, if such a common agency is not to institutionalize inefficiency it must apply at European level the principles set out in (2) to (10) above. In particular, the contractual relationship between such an agency and the companies has to clarify and separate responsibilities. An agency should define requirements in precise terms. The companies should have the responsibility for conceiving the best means of fulfilling them.

Despite all the potential snags in the MRCA and the important further tasks which lie ahead, its development together with the Jaguar and the Harrier provide the RAF with a solid programme of aircraft development and construction, after the years of upheaval and the cancellation of so many abortive national projects. It is important that the full potential of these aircraft be realized – and here a lesson can be learnt, not only from Dassault with his Mirage family, but also from such successful British aircraft as the Canberra, the Hunter and the Spitfire.

All these aircraft lasted many years, with the original plane giving birth to a whole family of variations fulfilling different roles. Both

56

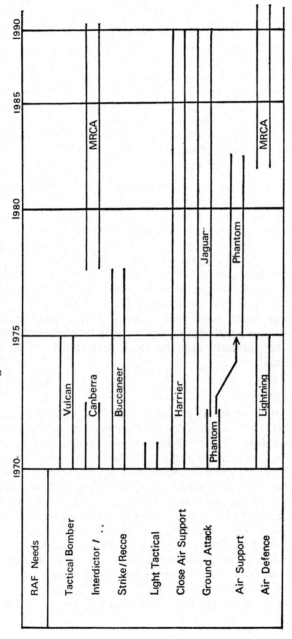

Chart B
Filling the RAF's Future Needs

the Jaguar and the MRCA have this potentiality. Indeed, together with the Harrier, versions of them might serve the bulk of the RAF's needs right through to 1990 and beyond (see Chart B).

For this reason, it would be both a waste of public funds and a damaging distraction for the aircraft industry if the Operational Requirements branch of the Ministry of Defence now settles down to devising new Operational Requirements for the 1980s which will soon be translated into new and expensive batch development programmes. A wholly different approach is needed at this time (1971), which, at the risk of repetition of what has gone before, should be summarized as follows:

(1) Effort must be concentrated on making the Jaguar, MRCA and Harrier successes, and on further developing these aircraft to fulfil the needs of the RAF and other European airforces. High priority in this work must be given to bringing Dassault back into the fold and combining the variable geometry programmes of the four major European nations.
(2) Meanwhile, at either European or national level, there should be some funding of single, advanced aerodynamic research prototypes as a means of keeping technology on the boil.
(3) Only when some new military need clearly emerges which provides a real opportunity to apply such new technology, should it be translated into the batch development of an operational aircraft.

CONCLUSION

This study of variable geometry aircraft development has ranged wide. It has shown that no-one in the Western world has yet mastered the problems of controlling the development and procurement of advanced-technology aircraft. In the US, complex, detailed control, vast resources and much paper have not succeeded in preventing gross cost escalation and major technical failure. In France, Dassault has produced a successful aircraft at low cost, but that aircraft does not have access to the major European markets; Dassault has won on technology but lost on politics. With the MRCA, Britain, Germany and Italy have achieved an important advance in the organization of European joint projects; but France and the experience and quality of Dassault are outside the venture, and the aircraft has yet to be proved and the bill to be paid.

If in the next few years Europe can find a way of combining some of the flair, simplicity and workmanlike approach of Dassault with the solid advance toward a common European effect embodied in Panavia, the expensive lessons of recent years may have been worthwhile.

Chapter 4
VEHICLE ENGINES:
DAVID AND GOLIATH

'When high-volume production is involved, cost reduction can be more profitable than new products unless they are really revolutionary.'

Companies visited:

General Motors (USA)
NSU (Germany)

The motor industry is not one in which major innovations succeed one another rapidly (as in, say, electronics). The Volkswagen still looks novel after 35 years. The gas turbine engine, first emerging during the last war, may become a serious commercial proposition in the early 1970s. Most cars still use the Otto-cycle piston engine which evolved in the early years of the century. Innovation is mainly concerned with constant minor developments of traditional designs and with fashion changes.

Yet, though innovation of a radical kind is rare, it can from time to time shift the economic pattern of the industry, for instance by enabling outsiders (like the Europeans in the American market) to shift established oligopolists. The following description of the efforts of two companies throws some light on this, on innovation practices generally, and on the use of QSES.

NSU AND THE WANKEL ROTARY ENGINE: A SMALL FIRM GRAPPLES WITH A FUNDAMENTAL INNOVATION
Phase I: Early History

In 1951, NSU was a very small technology-oriented firm employing some 4,000 people, whose main business was in motorcycles though they had been in the car business before 1929. Their own research and development department was already working successfully on new types of sliding-valve mechanisms, which contributed to the success of NSU motorcycles in competition during the 1950s.

In 1951, Herr Wankel, who had been a design engineer and innovator up to the war (by then with his own institution which

60

worked on aero-engines), was taken on as 'free collaborator' by the company. He got on well with the small NSU development team. In shattered postwar Germany they enabled him to get going again on his applied research, initially in his own house and garage, later in his own small institute.

James Watt was one of the earliest inventors to devise a rotary engine and since him there have been innumerable patents and inventions of varying complexity. None, however, has been seriously developed, despite the great inherent simplicity of the concept compared with a conventional piston engine. The main unsolved problem was the devising of a satisfactory seal which would prevent loss of compression.

Wankel's major contribution of principle was the idea that the sealing problem could be solved only by a flexible, sprung seal, and would never be solved merely by accurate machining. In 1954 he devised a triangular-shaped rotary piston within a figure-of-eight shaped cylinder: a conception much simpler than most previous rotary engines. No valves were needed.

Further elaboration of the principles was done by Professor Baier of the Technische Hochschule, Stuttgart, and others. The conception was tried out in pumps and compressors by NSU and in 1957 the first test engine ran.

Throughout this period the research and development team consisted essentially of one man, plus a few helpers, backed by the technically minded boss of NSU (Dr Ing G. S. von Heydekampf) and the chief engineer of NSU (von Frankenberger), who saw its potential as suggested by the NSU research engineer, Dr W. Froede.

Phase II: NSU's Crisis and Solution

Development of the Wankel engine, however, required larger resources. The concept had inherent advantages of simplicity, bringing less weight, smaller size, freedom from vibration, etc. But at least four major development problems had to be overcome:

(a) Putting into practice Herr Wankel's sealing principle (i.e. developing the mechanism, materials, etc.),
(b) lubrication (principles, systems testing, oil sealing, etc),
(c) cooling, and
(d) long life.

The crucial period for the Wankel engine, however, coincided with the collapse of NSU's motorcycle business (where the market was

61

shrinking fast, especially in Germany). Motorcycle turnover dropped from 185 million DM (say £16 million) in 1955 to 128 million DM (say £11 million) in 1958 and is virtually nothing today. With employment at 7,000 by 1958 and a total turnover of a mere 148 million DM, output per man dropped to under £2,000 per year. The company responded in the following way:

1. It diversified into car production and produced 127,000 in 1968, the year before the merger with the Auto Union Gmbh. Turnover reached 566 million DM (say £56 million) with employment of some 12,000, that is output per head of just under £5,000.

2. In 1958 a growing number of people in the company took the view that the Wankel development should be stopped since the company could not stand it – and the rest of the industry unanimously thought it was cranky. The chief executive, however, Dr von Heydekampf, took the categorical view that members of the company must back the Wankel engine or get out. The Wankel development team was built up steadily to 1960 to something like its 1970 size of some 35 engineers, in research, development and pre-production engineering, plus say 80 back-up staff, including draughtsmen, etc. Despite the doubts, the company attracted some bright young engineers interested in the work that was being done. Senior staff took a voluntary cut in salaries.

3. The company realized it must get licence revenue to finance development. No conventional car makers were interested, but the Curtiss-Wright Corporation, out of jet engines, and with a waning piston engine business, became the major North American partner in 1959. Curtiss-Wright got the arrangement off on the wrong foot initially, through premature publicity and internal troubles, but it eventually settled down.

By the early 1960s, despite the still scornful view of much of the motor industry, other important licensees came in and NSU by 1970 had 16 major licensees of whom the most active are Toyo Kogyo, Fichtel und Sachs, Daimler-Benz, Outboard Marine and Curtiss-Wright. (Rolls Royce, interested in military applications of the Wankel engine, and F. Perkins, in industrial uses, are UK licensees.) The licensees have been the major source of finance for further development. They are organized in a permanent patents pool in which all new patents based on the Wankel engine taken out by any member, are shared, free, with the others. There are regular meetings and a steady exchange of people among licensees.

This strategy has had the following effects:

(a) NSU of course will not be the sole exploiter of its remarkable work: a big company might well have kept it close to its chest and eventually reaped larger returns; however, apart from Citroen, and VW with whom NSU has since combined (see Phase III and IV below), there is as yet no European licensee in the small engine/ car range where NSU's chief interest lies.

(b) In addition to finance for development, the development of the engine has tapped a far wider range of brains – and this has certainly had value, for instance in exploring blind alleys at less cost to NSU.

4. At this stage the company did *not* seek massive outside funds in the form of a takeover, a major new shareholder or a big infusion of risk capital, though they did make a normal capital issue. And before 1968 no outsider *had ever* sought to take the company over, for the essential reason that the major motor companies have looked on the Wankel engine with scepticism ('Not Invented Here'?). Bank capital was, at that stage, expensive and hard to get in Germany. No government funds, of course, were available to help such R and D.

Here we should ask: if NSU had been a young innovating company in the United States would it have found it much easier to get risk capital? Were its management right to guard their independence carefully, accept capital restraints on internal growth and license widely?

The answer is that their approach diffused the knowledge more rapidly, to the benefit of the world's economy; it may conceivably have reduced the potential profit and productivity benefit for the company; but thanks to the inertia of the bulk of the world's motor industry and NSU's skill in licensing (each licensee gets a licence for particular areas and types of engine), no licensee has taken the bit between its teeth in the main areas competitive with NSU. Generous government support for R and D could have accelerated development and reduced dependence on licence revenue – but only if it had been given without excessive strings.

Phase III: into Production
The period since 1957 has been characterized by the following developments:

(1) Diversification into cars with conventional engines has been

successful and production had risen from nothing in 1957 to 127,000 units in 1968.

(2) The major problems of the Wankel engine have been overcome and it has been produced and used:

(a) in the NSU Spider sports car in 1963,
(b) in a limited number of outboard marine engines,
(c) by licensees Fichtel und Sachs AG for industrial purposes and by Toyo Kogyo for cars, and
(d) in the new RO80 car.

(3) In the early 1960s the almost universal scepticism began to change and the major licensees mentioned above came in. The specific criticisms from outside – that the problems of sealing, lubrication, long life, etc. could not be solved – gave way to a more general scepticism among the motor industry and broadening attempts by licensees to apply the Wankel engine to industrial applications.

(4) NSU has established with Citroen a joint company (COMOBIL) for the development and production of a Wankel-powered family car costing some £750.

Citroen will develop and manufacture the bodies and NSU the engines and transmission. The aim is to reach manufacture of some 500 units per day. Final assembly may be partly in France and partly in Germany.

Citroen's larger financial resources are being enlisted in the following ways:

A joint company (Comotor) with capital of 170 million Luxemburg francs (£15 million) has been set up on a 50–50 basis. This will produce the NSU-Wankel engines for the joint car and will be financed mainly by credits provided by Citroen. A new factory is under construction in the Saar region. Citroen will finance body development itself.

Investment in development of the specific motor, in plant, equipment and pre-production engineering is expected to cost some 150 million DM (£17 million).

(5) In the 1960s one major doubt concerned air pollution from the engine. This was successfully tackled, however, and it now appears that the engine has interesting characteristics which could turn out to be a selling point. The engine does not have better fuel economy than a conventional engine, but it is claimed to be smaller and lighter and therefore cheaper to produce.

Use of QSEs

The Wankel team grew between 1956 and 1960 and then stabilized. In 1967 it consisted of 27 graduates, plus 10 other QSEs and 100 others. At that stage, 19 of the graduates and 7 other QSEs were still in pure research.

By 1970, with commercial development of the engine well under way in the enlarged company, a much bigger effort was going into development and production engineering, as the table below shows.

The Wankel Team in 1970

	Graduates	Shop personnel	Total
Pure research	25	60	85
Development and production engineering	63	46	109
	88	106	194

Up till 1968 R and D on the Wankel engine was only costing some £500,000 (or 1 per cent of turnover) per year, but production engineering and investment are now mounting to a far higher figure.

Phase IV: Taken Over

With the year 1969 and the merger with the Auto Union GmbH. a new phase has set in. Through the merger with Auto Union, which was a 100 per cent subsidiary company of Volkswagen, Volkswagen became majority shareholder of the new company, AUDI NSU Union Aktiengesellschaft, on the basis of the relative market value of the merging firms. The new company was initially directed by a board under the continued presidency of Dr von Heydekampf.

The merger caused no change in realizing the plans for joint production of a car with Citroen. Since Citroen has joined the Fiat empire, the joint enterprise indirectly links the two giant European rivals, Fiat and Volkswagen, raising major questions for the future.

In the summer of 1970, General Motors announced its interest in buying shares of the Wankel GmbH. The NSU/Wankel patents are the joint property of AUDI NSU and the Wankel GmbH.; administration of the patents and licensing are managed together by AUDI NSU and the Wankel GmbH.

The new phase clearly showed that the world's giant automobile manufacturers, despite their earlier scepticism, no longer felt they

65

could afford the risk of another major company's succeeding with the Wankel engine. If GM succeeded in acquiring large numbers of Wankel shares, it could become, together with Volkswagen, one of the two largest shareholders controlling the Wankel patents. In 1970 it also bought a batch of Toyo Kogyo cars, the first small production cars to be marketed with Wankel engines. Toyo Kogyo has done important work on the seal problem.

Steady progress is being made with better materials for the Wankel engine; larger-scale production is bringing economies of scale and more efficient production methods. The problem of pollution, which was thought by GM in 1968 to be insuperable, has proved, at the least, to be no worse for the Wankel engine than for any other kind of internal combustion engine. The engineering problems involved are specific to the type of legislation introduced in different countries.

Assessment

In classic small-firm style NSU has broken through with a fundamental innovation. Single-mindedness and the interest of the project attracted good engineers during the 20-year haul. And though the company's profit record was poor, its management were skilful enough to keep the company afloat by diversification in the 1950s from motorcycles to cars, and by skilful licensing.

Because of its small size, apart from other reasons, output per man in NSU was, by the late 1960s, only half that of Volkswagen, though slightly better than that of British Leyland. When the Volkswagen takeover took place, production of the Ro80 was behind schedule because component supplies and production organization had not been up to expectation.

NSU thus had both a formidable innovation at its command and a need for stronger capabilities in marketing and in production organization, and more finance. It was a situation ripe for takeover by a company such as Volkswagen which had these strengths.

GENERAL MOTORS

General Motors, the world's largest company, employed some 757,000 workers in 1968 and had a turnover of $22·7 billion, giving it an output per man of $31,300 per year.

The Sloane Structure: the Balance between Divisions and Centre

A key feature of the company is the organizational principles

66

developed by Alfred P. Sloane: that is to say the establishment of separate operating divisions with a large measure of commercial independence, guided by a central system of financial control and services. That organizational structure, which helped to build up the company from a state of near collapse in 1921 to its present position, remains the main strength of General Motors. It was copied by most American companies decades ago; 50 years later it is being adopted by many British firms. In production and marketing this organization means a fair measure of commercial independence for the different car divisions, to the extent that they compete with each other (under central policy direction) and buying policies are competitive, with divisions buying from outsiders if GM production cannot compete.

It would be wrong to imagine, however, that GM's auto divisions operate as totally independent enterprises. The company's structure is designed to try to combine the maximum economies of scale in production with a market orientation which involves a great range of model variations and production facilities in different regions of the United States.

For instance, to achieve maximum economies of scale, the company points out that 'high-speed presses, with a single set of dies, produce inner door panels for all GM regular-sized cars'.

'Another example of efficiency is the integration of car assembly operations. Except for the Cadillac division, assembly operations by each car division of General Motors are integrated in part with some other car division. The fabrication of car bodies is the responsibility of Fisher Body Division. GM Assembly Division operates eight plants located throughout the country, and assembles not only the bodies but the complete vehicle. Furthermore each division depends on development efforts and production carried on in other divisions and on central staff activities, co-ordination and management.'[1]

In short, GM's divisional structure seeks to give divisions clear responsibility for a particular product, or service, to discipline the relations between divisions by commercial criteria, and within this framework to exploit, wherever possible, the economies of scale open to the company as a whole.

[1] *The Automobile Industry: a Case Study in Competition*, General Motors, October 1968.

Research and Development

In R and D a good deal of development and styling work is de-centralized to the divisions. But there is also a strong central research effort. The pressures to speed technology transfer from development to market are not, it seems, as strong as in firms like Texas Instruments and Ferranti in fast-moving technological industries.

GM's central research laboratory alone employs some 500 graduates and 1,000 others. It comprises 15 scientific and engineering departments and covers basic and applied research, from high-energy physics to the study of new polymers, through engineering research, including exploratory work on a wide range of engine conceptions, to fundamental mathematics and computer technology. Next to the research centre is a large *styling* staff which deals only with new car body development, an *engineering* staff which deals with the development of engineering products including new car chassis and engine development, and, most important, a *manu-facturing* staff, or more correctly manufacture development activity, concerned purely with research into cost-reducing manufacturing techniques. Since GM's many manufacturing divisions also do varying amounts of applied research and development, the total effort is formidable. The company put its spending on R and D in 1967 at $664 million or 3·3 per cent of turnover.

We cannot claim to have been able to make a detailed assessment of the largest company in the world in one short visit, but some features stand out.

(1) *Clear objectives.* Despite the vast size, there are clear *aims* for the different branches of the organization and they are spelt out clearly too. Those of the research laboratories, for instance, are defined publicly as:

(a) consultation to divisions,
(b) improvement of present products,
(c) development of new products, processes and materials,
(d) development of technical or scientific information, and
(e) establishment of a reputation of pre-eminence in science and technology.

(2) *GM policy on QSEs.* GM have long had a competent system of graduate recruitment followed by all-life training and career development of an orthodox kind:

(a) Since they cannot offer the independence of small fast-growing

68

companies to graduates, they offer security ('as good as at a university'). This is important since universities, backed by government research contracts, now pay as much as industry. The graduate staff of the research laboratories is growing slowly (6 per cent average over 10 years), not spectacularly, and has a low turnover.

(b) Standard recruiting from the universities, they believe, tends to bring in only average people. To get the high-fliers, they take on university professors as technical consultants so that these get interested in the company and steer their best students toward it. They follow this up in research by putting really good academic people in charge of departments, whom other researchers respect. After salaries, they regard this as the most important condition for keeping research workers happy.

(c) There is a corporation-wide tuition refund plan, with fees re-imbursed. Occasionally, bright B.Sc.s of Ph.D. calibre are given unpaid leave to get their doctorates; half come back, half become professors. Supervisors may attend annual management training refresher courses. From time to time, more senior executives are sent (paid) to 10–12 week business management courses.

(d) One serious problem is that research scientists (in conjunction with universities and high-technology industries) get paid more than production engineers. So, as in some British companies in the past, there is serious difficulty in transferring R and D teams into production.

(3) This, and the centralized research setup, might be expected to create the kind of blockage in the flow of information and people between research and production which has caused so much waste of brainpower in Britain. But, to some extent, this is mitigated by the vigorous emphasis which GM management place on eventual profit-ability. There has been no attempt to do what Ford have attempted and abandoned: to set up what is virtually a university where researchers can explore whatever field they like. Thus, though there is basic research, it must have some apparent eventual application: solid state physics leading to better materials; mathematics to better computer systems. In the words of Lawrence Hafstad, former vice-president for research: 'Industry . . . must do basic research. But they should do only enough basic research to keep their applied research healthy.' The most vital part of the research effort seems to be in what is called 'service divisions', i.e. overcoming an engineering

or consumer problem, and the huge and vital manufacturing staff developing cost-reduction techniques.

Not Invented Here

At the time of our visit we were indeed deeply impressed by General Motors' scepticism, at least in automobiles, of fundamental innovation. Years ago, they explain, under Charles Kettering, GM's research laboratories developed the locomotive diesel engine, Freon, the key to the refrigerator industry, high octane gasolines, and so on. They have also, over the years, shown a capability for developing new business – refrigerators, defence.

But in the car industry, as the record shows, major change has often come from outside pressure. GM made considerable efforts to stop Ralph Nader from opening up the safety question, which has involved them in major development work and innovation. The stagnant pattern of basic car design (the front-engined, rear-wheel drive, Otto-cycle-engined large car) has been modified only in responce to vigorous European competition.

In the engine field, GM are actually doing work on a very wide range of engines – and in May 1969 produced an impressive public display of 19 different types of automotive power, ranging from the Stirling engine, under licence from Philips, to the gas turbine and the free piston engine, and electric-powered vehicles. All but one of these products, however, in GM's own analysis, at that time still fell short of commercial viability. GM claims, for instance, that because of its complexity the steam engine costs up to three times as much as the conventional piston engine. The view is not shared by the US government committee, chaired by Professor Morse, which has also investigated many types of power plants. It put steam engine costs at only 1·5 times that of conventional plant; Professor Morse is so convinced of the viability of steam that he has since gone into the steam engine business.

The gas turbine is one major exception to GM's commercial rejection of new engine types. GM began developing turbines over 20 years ago. The work will culminate with the production in 1971 of a commercial turbine engine for heavy-duty vehicles, by the Detroit diesel division. During these years GM has produced five generations of turbines and a number of turbine-powered buses, trucks and cars.

In GM's assessment, the gas turbine still offers less fuel economy than the diesel engine. But it is lighter, vibration-free, and can run on a variety of fuels. It causes little pollution and has big growth poten-

70

tial. As with so many innovations, a combination of competitive pressures, plus a general advance of the technology to the level where it is becoming potentially profitable, has prompted more than one world manufacturer to take the commercial plunge at the same time.

As for the Wankel engine, before 1970 GM had neither done research on it nor taken a licence from NSU. GM held that its tendency to produce excessive pollution made development not worthwhile. Only when commercial application of the engine on a large scale, through Volkswagen or Citroen, drew near, did GM seek a stake. To sum up, the view of the manager of GM's research laboratory on engines in 1968 was that: 'The auto engine will remain basically the same as it is now for the rest of the century, chiefly because it is easy to build and maintain. It may be developed and stretched but not fundamentally changed or supplanted.' Or in the words of the director of research: 'When high-volume production is involved, cost reduction can be more profitable than new products unless they are really revolutionary.'

Why does GM present the apparent paradox of an immense research and development capability side by side with an apparent lack of enthusiasm for radically new products? Does the contrast with NSU simply reflect the, by now, familiar ecology of organizations: big ones reluctant to innovate, small ones providing a more favourable environment for thrusting new ideas?

One hypothesis might be that in an ologopolistic situation, i.e. one where there are few suppliers, with GM the largest, the company's interest is to maximize its profits by maintaining prices of existing products through the exercise of price leadership. This type of hypothesis was implicit in some of the questions posed in the Select Committee on Small Business of the United States Senate in October 1968. General Motors produced some impressive answers: they pointed out that GM had acquired its present market position, not by acquisition, but by a competitive effort which had pushed up its market share from 14 per cent in 1921 to a peak of 52 per cent in 1962 (48 per cent in the first eight months of 1968). A constant process of innovation in small matters (materials, lubricants, computerization of design and calculations on stress, and so on) had improved the product and brought the price down. New car prices had risen 22 per cent and compensation per man-hour by 51 per cent – and so on.

There is no doubt that the cruder version of the oligopoly argument falls down in face of the constant competitive development

71

of the US car market. But there is no doubt too that the innovative challenges – the small car, the Wankel engine, front-wheel drive – have come from outside the colossus of the industry.

The observation made by GM itself on the profitability of fundamental innovations, ought to be underlined. The largest company, which obtains the biggest economies of scale and hence high profits from existing products, has a strong interest in cost-reducing improvements in production techniques which further strengthen its position. Small companies which are having difficulty in competing in the big league for existing products have a bigger incentive to try to enlarge their market share by innovating radically new products. There is therefore some commercial logic in the pattern whereby smaller enterprises make major innovations while the largest adopt a waiting strategy, keeping themselves abreast of world-wide technical change, but concentrating on improvement in production techniques until the time comes when competition forces them to change products fundamentally. For the large company the danger is that habitual inertia may make it unable to change quicky enough in response to competitive challenge. For the public interest there can be damage if the larger company, slow to innovate itself, takes over a smaller innovation, not to develop it, but to suppress it.

It will be interesting to see which concern – Volkswagen–NSU, GM or another licensee – first makes a commercial success of the Wankel engine.

Chapter 5

ELECTRONICALLY CONTROLLED KNITTING MACHINERY: NEW ENTERPRISE IN AN OLD INDUSTRY

Companies visited:
Bentley Engineering Group (UK)
Franz Morat (West Germany)

The knitting machinery industry is 200 years old and has been evolving throughout this time by means of continuous, detailed improvements by the freemasonry of knitters. The basic machine is, in a sense, a machine tool, plus some 20 per cent of its value in the form of the highly specialized needles, cams, cylinders and elements where the skill of the knitting machine technician comes in.

No-one can accuse this industry of not being conscious of the market for their product, or its use. This is an intensely fashion-bound industry. The showrooms of the three principal Bentley companies simply show clothes and garments made from the machines. Machines have constantly to be varied to suit customers' changing needs. All this, however, tends to orient the industry toward flexibility in detailed minor improvements and away from fundamental change.

Before the war the leading exporter was Germany, followed by the USA, followed by Britain. The German industry was concentrated round Chemnitz in the Soviet zone and the Russians have essentially destroyed this nucleus. Refugees have redeveloped the industry in some measure in the West. Karl Mayer, who crossed with a rucksack in 1948, has, for instance, built up an enterprise which totally commands the world market for warploom machines; his recipe has been tremendous personal entrepreneurial energy, a hard-working labour force, and the design and production of a tough machine, simpler and cheaper than anyone else put on the market.

But in knitting machines Germany has not recovered its pre-eminence, giving the British industry the chance (against vigorous opposition) to fill the gap.

The US industry has lost its prewar share of world markets. The basic problem is lack of the kind of skilled labour still needed in knitting machinery manufacture. Management mistakes also played a part. But above all, high us wage rates are not compensated in this industry, as yet, by more advanced and capital intensive production methods (except in some areas, such as foundries). A good many us machines therefore sell only behind high American protective tariffs and are not as advanced as European models.

BENTLEY ENGINEERING: A NEW FORWARD LOOK

The Bentley Engineering Group, owned by Sears Holdings (Charles Clore's holding company), has brought together a number of companies over a period of time and now consists of twelve member companies of which the principal three are William Cotton (straight bar and 'V' bend machinery for outerwear), Bentley Engineering (sock and stocking single jersey and interlock machines) and Wildt, Mellor, Bromley (circular knitting machines of the jacquard double jersey and garment type). The Group turnover in 1968 was £35 million, with a manpower of 10,000.

Until 1965, a member of the Bentley family was managing director and there was no fundamental development activity, just the constant improvement of machines; virtually no graduates were employed. The firm took some knocks from innovating rivals (especially when, as with the Italian Billi stocking machine, a concentrated and well-conceived effort was made in a narrow field).

In 1966, however, a change in managing director took place and a new common development company for the Group was set up. The new managing director, Mr John Wegerif, had a much wider engineering background. Whereas in many industries we have seen that a main need was to relate development closely to the market, here the need was felt to be to create a development group sufficiently detached from the endless pressures of fashion to think about more fundamental innovation. Peter Findlay, a former aircraft engineer from Rolls Royce, was put in charge. This appointment has already begun to open the eyes of established textile engineers. Split-second photography, and strain gauging, for instance, used in the aircraft industry, have been invaluable helps in studying needle and thread movements.

In 1969 the development company employed some 47 people, 4 of them mechanical engineering graduates and textile graduates, 1 HND and 8 HNC. There were 20 in experimental shops in each of the three manufacturing companies and, in addition, development work is carried out in the factories. Altogether some £1 million (say 3 per cent of the turnover) was spent on R and D. In all this Charles Clore plays a helpful part, in contrast to some other parent companies. He leaves the running of his companies to his managing directors, provided the profits come in. Provided they can pay the interest he is ready to supply abundant capital, and indeed his pressure is toward heavier investment, especially in development.

The new push in the Bentley Group has firmly re-established it in a predominant position. Of the output, 75 per cent is exported.

Wildt, Mellor, Bromley is easily the largest supplier of circular knitting machines in the world.

FRANZ MORAT: A SMALL MAN WITH A FUNDAMENTAL INNOVATION

The most interesting challenge to Wildt, Mellor, Bromley's knitting predominance comes from Franz Morat, a south German business-man.

Phase I: Entering the Industry

In 1946 Herr Morat took a partnership in a small firm (Hellige) to manufacture medical electronic apparatus. His production manager (Richard Schmidt) was a mechanical engineer and his head of R and D (Dr J. A. Schaeder) a physicist. These two saw the relevance of electronics to the textile industry. Stitching could be recorded digitally, as on a cardiogram, and impulses transmitted to the needles. With the clear intention of developing electronically controlled knitting machines, Morat sold his share in the business (Hellige) in 1953 to Lytton Industries and invested the proceeds in developing a textile machinery business, which initially employed some 50 people. At first he remained chief executive of Hellige, supplementing his slim financial resources.

Schmidt learnt not textile engineering but the more limited area of knitting machine engineering. By 1964 the firm was marketing a successful 30-inch conventional jacquard knitting machine at a sufficient profit to be able to finance their dream innovation. Turn-over at that time was some 8 million DM (£700,000) (say 200 machines per year at that time) and the conception of electronic control was clearly worked out. The higher costs of the development phase, however, remained to be paid for.

Phase II: Expansion and Development

Since 1964, the turnover of the company has risen from 8 million DM to an estimated 50 million DM (say £5 million) in 1969, and the labour force to 700 (i.e. an output per man of some £7,000 per year or twice the Bentley figure). Exports comprise 80 per cent of turnover and of this half is in the new electronic machine put on the market in 1967. The degree of success has enabled Morat to finance development of his electronically controlled machine partly out of current profits.

Development, he estimates, cost 3–5 million DM or, say, £500,000 over 5 years, i.e. some 5 per cent of turnover. Half of this has come out of profits and half from outside – from the Swiss firm of Sulzer whom he brought in as joint partner, to raise the basic capital of the company from 2 to 4 million DM.

The development team consisted originally of 3 people and had grown to 20 by 1969 (including 6 engineers and 1 physicist).

There are some 10 qualified engineers in the rest of the company (mostly from the equivalent of good technical colleges) and only one is a graduate textile engineer. He is in marketing.

Training consists of a company apprenticeship scheme, management training courses by correspondence, and short courses in knitting and electronics application. In particular the firm's electrolab gives courses to the firm's non-graduate service engineers (of whom there are some 20 throughout the world) in servicing electro-control systems.

What is the Morat Innovation?

The basic conception was to record a pattern digitally, store it and then transmit it to the machine. In a normal knitting machine the information is basically stored on the needle discs – which, because of size, can plainly only accommodate say up to 120 different needle variations. An electronic storage of some kind can have an infinitely complex pattern and instead of changing 1,280 discs on a machine, you change only one film.

One basic prototype was built, then 10 which were tried out on nearby customers and much amended, then 20, and then continuous standard production took place. In 1969 some 200 standard, electronic, 36-feed machines costing about £14,000 each were delivered. Until 1969 production was in the garage phase of development, in a jumble of bursting sheds.

The present 36-feed inch machine is definitely more expensive than equivalent conventional designs. Its advantage is that designs can be changed quickly (just change the film and the spools) and can be far more sophisticated. (The films, however, have to be obtained from Morat.) It is therefore ideal for patterning and trying out designs, one in each textile firm, but is much more expensive than conventional machines.

In 1970 a first small-scale computer input for the machine was put on the market. Using this, films can be dispensed with. A scanner will look at a design and the computer will translate this direct into the machine. The designs will be recorded on tape and can be kept. The computer development has been commissioned from Philips.

During 1970 construction of a new factory with five times the capacity of the old one was completed (cost, some £1,400,000) and turnover was expected to be over 100 million DM (£12 million) in 1971. Morat will then be producing some 1,000 machines per year: a little less than Wildt, Mellor, Bromley, the largest in the world in the field, were doing in 1969, but half their expected output in 1971–72.

The key question is at what point the machine becomes competitive in price for normal production (i.e. not just patterning).

BENTLEY AND ELECTRONICS

The Bentley Group have reacted to the challenge by working with Newmark Engineering, an electronic company with a background in aviation and weapons control, on their own electronic system. Though their own development team is larger than Morat's, they hold the view that it is best to enlist electronic capability outside.

Their commercial policy is to continue at present selling conventional machines (which they are doing very successfully) so long as the Moratronik is uncompetitive on price (except for patterning), and to prepare to enter the market in 1972–73 with their more advanced electronic machine, which they believe will have much higher productivity than competing machines.

This policy is not just British dilatoriness (cf. fast reactors). Bentley mechanical jacquard machines are simple to maintain and have sold out into 1974. They consider that most knitting mills will not be ready to deal with the complicated maintenance of electronics before 1973. Whether the Bentley strategy succeeds will depend on how fast Morat continues to develop his system and brings down the price.

Clearly the knitting machine industry is entering a new phase in which basic development is going to have increasing importance.

Bentley intend to step up the size of the Bentley development company rapidly and to make a systematic effort to ensure that their dynamism infects their member companies, by moving people in and out of it. They see they should recruit more graduates, but also find problems in fitting them into industrial life. They believe it would work better if undergraduates could spend a year in the firm before their final year, or before university (a form of sandwich course, one might say, but not so compressed and, they would add, without the reputation of a lower standard which still attaches to sandwich courses). They are developing a closer relation with Loughborough University of Technology; the Bentley Group managing director is a member of the University Council and the Group have founded a Chair there.

Electronic control of the individual machine must lead on to whole systems of machines jointly controlled, but there are major problems of 'plumbing' – finding a way to feed the thousands of threads to the machines continuously without human intervention and with synchronized machine speeds. The needle itself has now become the limiting factor in knitting speeds and more research is needed here.

There is plainly big scope, too, for radically improving production methods of knitting machinery, for instance in the direction of Molins-type automated batch production of components. Labour productivity at Morat is, it seems, much higher. There are no demarcation problems, for instance, in moving knitters on to electronic work. All the Bentley design teams are busy reducing the labour content of the product. In addition, special-purpose machine tools are being installed in increasing numbers. Bentley have created a Group production engineering section to review their manufacturing methods and policies on a Group basis in the light of the development of more sophisticated machine tools.

CONCLUSION

Textile machinery, like machine tools, is an industry in which, because of the high degree of manual skill involved, Europe can continue to lead the United States (even in output per man), in an era of much higher productivity and automation. It is an industry where the British firm concerned really does have the market orientation which is lacking in some of our other examples. The textile machinery companies are already beginning to design their customers' factories (though more could be done here). The growing development effort fits into the right environment.

But it will have to be stepped up rapidly. As in numerically controlled machine tools, we have seen the value, in these examples, of transfer of technology from the high technology industries (aircraft, electronics). But these new technologies and systems have got to penetrate not merely the machinery firms, but also the textile mills themselves, which are not yet ready for electronics and automation. And plainly this process of transfer requires the spearhead high-technology industries to exist already.

The need for sustained care and effort in transferring technology into an old established industry, is brought home by the sharp contrast between the successful example of Franz Morat and that of Evershed and Vignoles, a British manufacturer of naval equipment (including electronics) which spent £300,000 in the early 1960s, together with an inventor, MacQueen, on developing a tape-controlled flat on V-bed garment machine. Extensive market surveys were carried out and expert knitting machine engineers were brought in during the drawing stages, but the designers had no background of experience in the textile machinery industry of the kind acquired by Morat. Finances dried up before a reliable machine had been fully developed and the project was dropped.

The Morat example is a classic illustration of the innovating small firm which proves that it is possible to innovate significantly from a very narrow base, provided you specialize judiciously. Small size in this case makes it possible to operate efficiently with absolutely no administrative tail (though the buying in of a large number of specialized parts – needles, electronic circuits, etc. – explains part of the high turnover per man; this is an assembly industry). Perhaps one should also add that the heroic age of the German postwar entrepreneur – with its many qualities in common with early nineteenth-century Britain – did owe much to a tax system with maximum personal rates of 55 per cent. This, together with the primitive character of the capital market, encouraged the continuance of the private company.

Morat's main aim is not to make money, but he will not be unhappy if he eventually gets a substantial return from his years of effort. He has already graduated to the second phase of the small innovating enterprise: partnership with a larger supplier of capital. It will be interesting to see how he tackles the wider management tasks of organizing and controlling a larger concern.

Chapter 6

PILKINGTONS AND THE FLOAT-GLASS PROCESS: FIRST OF THE FEW

'Pilkingtons not only invent, but do things with the result.'

Companies visited:
Pilkington Brothers (UK) and licensees (US)

The development of the float-glass process by Pilkingtons is one of the classic innovatory success stories of British industry. Until the advent of the float-glass process, there were two methods of continuously manufacturing flat transparent glass:

(a) The sheet process in which a ribbon is drawn upward from a free surface of molten glass. This process was developed by Fourcault, Pittsburgh Plate Glass and Libby-Owens-Ford and gave a product which is relatively low in cost, has a fire-polished surface but is relatively poor in optical distortion.

(b) The polished plate process used since the middle of the seventeenth century in which a ribbon of glass is either cast or rolled. In the 1920s and 1930s this was improved mainly by Pilkingtons, through the use of a furnace for continuous casting and through better grinding and polishing techniques. It gives a product with a high cost and a non-fire-polished surface but with good optical distortion characteristics.

For a very long time glass makers have tried to find a way of casting glass so smoothly that it will not need grinding and polishing. As early as 1901 a patent was taken out in the USA for a process which used a bath of molten metal, but the technology at that stage did not make it possible even to try it out. Latter attempts included the use of steam-cushioned rollers to avoid marking the surface, and vibrating plattens. None of these was successful.

Pilkingtons found the answer. In 1952 Alastair Pilkington first conceived the notion of using liquid tin as the platform on which to form a ribbon of molten glass, and then using the tin to support the ribbon until fire-finished surfaces set sufficiently hard to be handled without damage. Tin was chosen because of its relatively high boiling point and low melting point, its non-toxicity and the fact that it could be kept free of oxide by using a carefully controlled atmosphere. By good fortune it turned out that the equilibrium between gravity and surface tension for the tin/glass system gave a ribbon which was 7 mm thick. Sixty per cent of the flat glass trade was in glass 6 mm thick and it was relatively easy, by stretching the ribbon of glass, to reduce its equilibrium thickness from 7 mm to the required 6 mm. Great problems faced metallurgists, chemists and physicists who then had to invent a whole new technology. Chemists had to grapple with the problem of surface oxidation of the tin spoiling the glass surface. Engineers and the team generally had to devise the right conditions and machinery for pouring the molten glass and forming ribbons of glass to the required widths.[1] Scaling up from the initial pilot plant to a full-scale production process brought further new problems.

By 1959, however, after 7 years of development work, commercial glass was being produced. The construction of a second plant and the conversion of a third brought total investment in the new process to £9 million within the first 10 years.

The process has had a dramatic impact on the world's flat-glass industry, whose turnover is worth some £500 million per year. The capital cost of a plate-glass production line was reduced by one-third in relation to output. Overall manufacturing costs were reduced by a quarter. By 1970 the float process had almost completely superseded the plate-glass process throughout the world and was starting to make inroads into the thicker end of sheet-glass manufacture. Some sixteen licences have been taken out, licensees including all the world's major glass producers. Pilkingtons' cumulative licence revenue reached over £25 million by 1970.

One should add one other notable feature of the Pilkington success story. The process was conceived and developed by Pilkingtons and they have reaped major rewards. Often the inventor of a process or product does not reap the main benefits; often, too, innovative efforts of major importance, such as this, are conducted in more than one company at a time.

HOW IT HAPPENED

The float-glass innovation took place in a company that was then of

[1] For a full technical account of the innovation see Sir Alastair Pilkington's paper to the Royal Society (*Proceedings*, Series A314). See also K. J. B. Earle, 'The Development of the Float Glass Process and the Future of the Glass Industry', *Chemistry and Industry*, 1967.

medium size but small enough for all the key technical employees to know each other and be linked by easy and informal communications. Most of them were concentrated in the St Helens area.

In the ethos of the company, set by the owning family, all technical employees were part of a common technical team. Technical competence carried authority in its own right. People were discouraged, indeed prevented, from using their status to shout other people down.

This was a company whose leaders cared about technology, especially since the company was caught off balance at one point in the 1920s with obsolete equipment. In the past Pilkingtons had made significant technical contributions to grinding and polishing plate glass. In 1950 it was spending about £300,000 on R and D or 3 per cent of a turnover of some £10 million. It was employing about 31 graduates in the company research department and about 20 more scattered in development teams attached to the production divisions.

In 1952 Alastair Pilkington (a cousin of the family) was working in the plate-glass division as production manager. He had previously worked in the sheet-glass division; the contrast between the cheapness of the sheet process and the expense of the plate process, with its high electric power costs in rolling and grinding (5,000 horsepower needed for one plant), helped to focus his mind on the search for a way to make smooth plate more cheaply.

After mentally exploring various alternative approaches, he hit on the tin-float idea and committed it to paper. From that time on Alastair Pilkington's forceful personality continued to be the driving force behind the idea.

Alastair Pilkington's immediate superior, the production director of the flat-glass group (which included both plate and sheet), was quickly attracted by the idea. So was the company's main board. The board saw the immense potential economic return from the idea and from this time on backed it with large sums of money. Their basic approach was that they would continue to do so unless it was proved to be impossible. The board was also willing to cut across any organizational boundaries in the company to put the concept into practice.

The board's vigorous support and the awareness that they were handling an idea with high potential return for effort gave the development team which was set up a powerful motivation: a sense of the importance and excitement of their task.

A small project group was set up in 1952 which consisted basically of 3 people, Richard Barradell-Smith and 2 graduates. Barradell-Smith was at the time manager of the development team in the plate-glass works, but the project group worked in the sheet-glass factory in order to be able to make use of molten glass prepared for a rolling process. The group reported directly to Alastair Pilkington.

The technique used was to build two small pilot plants, one after the other, incorporating successive improvements. The first simply made 10-inch wide plates of glass and cost £5,000; the second was a continuous 48-inch plant costing £100,000. The work itself was done by the very small project team working in the production shops, but they drew on other people's brains and ideas, interrogating people in the basic research department for instance.

In 1957 the project group believed they were capable of building a production plant and the work entered a new phase. The team was expanded to between 6 and 8 people, 2 to 3 graduates of various disciplines and 4 to 5 HNC. It moved back into the plate-glass factory and built what was expected to be the first commercial plant at a cost of £1·4 million. At this stage the work became, if anything, more multi-disciplinary. The contribution of the pure scientists increased, as individuals from the research department were brought in to help on problems such as construction materials, heating and atmosphere control and preventing the glass from running out. At the same time the full commercial disciplines were brought to bear as warehousemen and glass handlers, marketing and marketing development departments, became involved.

Major chemical and physical problems had still to be overcome, however. For 14 months the new plant produced glass which was unsaleable (70,000 tons of it) because of internal faults. Then suddenly, saleable glass was produced. After a few months the plant was refurbished and unsaleable glass poured out once again. After very careful analysis, the team discovered that a fault in the apparatus had played a key part in the initial success. The effect of the damage was simulated in the production plant and from this time on (1959) commercial glass was produced on a large scale and the development never looked back.

This second phase (1957–59) was remarkable in a number of ways. It tested the resolution of the board, who spent a further £1·4 million before the new plant produced commercial glass. It demonstrated also what some call luck and others would call the ability to learn from accident – often a characteristic of successful radical innovation.

A further plant was built in 1962 and another converted in 1963, to

G

bring total expenditure on development and first exploitation to £9 million in 10 years.

REASONS FOR SUCCESS

To sum up, the major reasons for Pilkington's success in carrying a radical innovation from invention, through development, to commercial exploitation, were:

1. There was a clear objective and an idea to fulfil it.
2. The board rapidly recognized the economic value of the idea and showed a sustained willingness to back it with money, so long as it was not proved to be impossible.
3. There was a willingness to cut across any conventional organization lines in the company to put it into practice.
4. Those involved recognized the high potential return from their efforts and hence had a driving motivation.
5. There was a long-standing belief in scientific ideas as a basis for action. Pilkingtons set up a central research laboratory well before the war. By 1952 R and D was costing the company £300,000 per year, which has since risen to £3 million (4 per cent of turnover). R and D and the technical department employ about 5 per cent of the company's personnel. But, as one US licensee put it: 'Pilkingtons not only invent, but do things with the results.'
6. Above all, a major organizational feature of the Pilkington innovation distinguished it sharply from those of many of the other companies discussed in these studies. The development was carried out, not in the central research laboratory, but in the production shop, in the factory environment. Indeed, the central research department made a relatively small contribution to the float-glass innovation, in the initial stages.

The product development groups attached to production divisions indeed form the spearhead of Pilkingtons' technical policy. There are central research and development laboratories; the research laboratories have 180 graduate QSEs and the development laboratories have 100. They conduct research on sands and compose new materials. But in addition each product division has a team of anything from 10 to 30 graduate QSEs and perhaps as many with HND or HNC who are working on improving current technology. In process improvement the market for a new process is within the company's own workshops which use the process. Acceptance by production staff of new glass

84

technology is best gained by having the new technology developed under their noses.

7. All this took place in a company large enough to be able to finance the innovation, but small enough for the leading technical people to have easy, good communications. The conception of the float process, the decision to try it and the execution of the project all happened on a small front – and the decisions were made by discussion among relatively few people.

This small-business technique has inevitably given way to more systematic organization as the company's R and D spending has grown, and development groups in each division have acquired a life of their own. In 1950 there were altogether only 20 people in the works development teams and it was easy to keep communications going on an informal basis. Twenty years later, with 5 product divisions and 250 QSEs distributed about them, systematic appraisal of development possibilities and some central direction of development projects is essential. Recommendations for development policy, product changes and technical policy are formulated by technical working parties for each particular area of operations (e.g. annealing, warehousing, melting). They are passed to the technical advisory committee of the general board. This committee formulates policy and passes it to the technical executive committee for implementation. Since some of the same people are on the working party and on both committees, communication and follow-up are good. But rather more paper and rather more time would probably be spent today on a decision to translate the modern equivalent of float from idea to execution than was spent in the early 1950s.

A financial comment by Lord Pilkington, the company's chairman, is also worth recording here. Shortly before Pilkingtons' very successful first public share issue, in 1970, he remarked that if Pilkingtons had gone public 15 years before, it is doubtful whether its resources would have been available to develop float glass. It was one thing to play for high stakes with family money; quite another to put at risk the funds of the shareholding public.

DIFFUSION OF THE INNOVATION

Once Pilkingtons had mastered the float-glass process in 1959, they were in possession of an innovation with the potential to transform the world's glass industry and their own position in it. Strategic decisions had then to be made on how best to exploit it.

85

In the British market they already controlled 90 per cent of the market through direct sales and through their close relationship and subsequent takeover (in 1955) of Triplex Safety Glass, the major suppliers to the motor industry. If there had been a serious British competitor to Pilkingtons in 1959 (BIG, the small producer of safety glass promoted by Ford and BMC as an alternative British source of supply in fact proved too small to be viable), it would have had difficulty in surviving a Pilkington attack.

In the world market Pilkingtons had, in theory, three major options open to it: to concentrate on direct exports, relying on the price competitiveness of the new process to carve out a larger share of world markets; to invest in capacity abroad; or to license.

At this point it is worth recalling the structure of the world's glass industry. This is a classic oligopolistic industry, that is to say one dominated by a few large producers. The world's major glass producers are shown in Table 6. Geology and geography play some part in the structure of the industry. An ideal location for a glass industry is one situated near supplies of good iron-free sand, a source of soda-ash, quarries for dolomite and limestone, a cheap source of fuel and a major port. South-west Lancashire is one of these locations and gave birth to Pilkingtons. The Meuse basin in Southern Belgium and Northern France is another, providing a base for the Continental leaders, Saint Gobain and Glavabel. Was Pilkingtons to attack world markets direct, by export or direct investment, or to license?

To appreciate the climate in which the decision was taken it is worth recalling that the Monopolies Commission, in its report[2] on the flat-glass industry, in 1968 described two informal agreements between Pilkingtons and Continental glass producers. One, the 'Sheet-Glass Entente', prepared in 1956, laid down agreed export quotas, prices and conditions of sales in world markets outside the signatories' home markets and in the United Kingdom. In the words of the Monopolies Commission's report:

'Although the agreement has never been signed, we are told by Pilkingtons that its provisions have been loosely observed. We have no information from [the Continental] producers about their attitude to the draft agreement, but the extent to which they observe common prices here in the UK suggests that they may pay some regard to its provisions in the United Kingdom market.'

[2] The Monopolies Commission, *Flat Glass*, HMSO, 1968.

A second agreement concerns float/plate. Once a year Pilkingtons and the Continental producers meet and agree on the aggregate quantity discounts to be allowed to particular UK customers. This must involve providing detailed information on each other's sales. The companies also inform each other in advance of price changes. These understandings are not binding; if they were some would almost certainly contravene Article 85 of the Rome Treaty. They do, however, enshrine an accepted spirit of price leadership and an historical tradition.

In this situation it is hardly surprising that Pilkingtons decided on what the company calls an 'orderly' diffusion of the innovation, that is to say to license it to other major producers and not to start a price-cutting war. It did this on the following grounds:

1. When the process was announced in 1959, Pilkingtons were aware that it still contained great scope for further development; at that time, for instance, Pilkingtons had still only made one thickness of float glass (6 mm); they believed further development would come faster if other licensees shared in the process, feeding back their ideas. All the licence agreements provide that Pilkingtons will receive back any development made by licensees and that future developments of the process by Pilkingtons will automatically be shared too. In practice it has been Pilkingtons whose head start has enabled them to develop techniques for manufacturing other thicknesses of float and indeed to develop further major improvements in the process, such as the electro-float process.[3] But there has been a useful flowback of information from the licensees (licensees have patented over 100 new developments) and in one case at least (Ford's innovation of lining the bath with carbon) the licensee has made a significant advance.

2. By comparison with some of the world's giants, Pilkingtons was still a relatively small company which needed to maximize early return on its big investment in float in order to invest in further development of the process, in expansion of production at home, and in a limited expansion of production facilities in its stronger markets abroad. In 1960 the company's capital assets were worth some £20 million and its turnover some £50 million. It felt it was not in a position to raise sufficient capital to invest in major production facilities throughout the world.

[3] Metallic ions are electrolysed into the glass, using the tin in the bath as a cathode.

In 1959 Pilkingtons therefore informed all major glass producers in the Western world that it was prepared to license the process to them. All have since taken out licences, as have Czechoslovakian and Russian manufacturers. The licence agreements contain no exclusive provisions to limit the market in which licensees can operate – with one exception. The terms have given Pilkingtons formidable royalties (in one case, for instance, $120,000 for each float line built, $1,200,000 for the initial disclosure of information and then a 6 per cent royalty on sales for 8 years and 4 per cent for the next 8). These arrangements have brought in a licence revenue of over £25 million in the first 10 years; with investment in world

Table 5

Pilkingtons' Licence Revenue and Profits (1969/70)
(£'000, year ending 31 March)

	Lump sum[a] licensing receipts	Licensing income[b] and technical fees, less related expenditure	Total profit before tax	Group turnover
1963	1,400		6,466	60,950
1964	1,850		7,251	67,371
1965	1,650	(44)	9,440	81,004
1966	450	894	7,320	84,850
1967	175	2,177	8,425	86,320
1968	625	3,856	11,804	97,552
1969	525	5,883	18,366	113,378
1970	275	6,729	14,074[c]	116,894

a. Initial payments for knowhow, credited, after tax, to capital reserves.
b. Mainly % royalties on turnover.
c. Hit by strike.

Source: Accountants' Report to Pilkington Brothers and J. Schroeder Wagg, in Pilkingtons' Prospectus, November 1970.

float capacity rising to a value of some £200 million by the end of 1970 Pilkingtons expects to have received some £100 million in royalties by 1980. Already by 1970 licence revenue was responsible for well over a third of the company's profits.

Licensing helped to give Pilkingtons the resources to expand production at home, increase exports and embark on the development of overseas manufacturing capacity in what can only be described as 'Pilkington territory' or neutral ground – that is to say, not in the home markets of major overseas competitors. In North America, though there was no attempt to invest inside the US market, two major float plants have been built in Canada which supply the Canadian motor industry and export across the border. Sheet plants have been built in Canada, South Africa, Australia, India, New Zealand, Argentina and, together with an associate, in Mexico. Float plants are planned for the 1970s in Australia, South Africa and Argentina.

Sales from overseas companies were worth some £22 million by 1969, and their capital assets some £40 million, compared with £100 million in the UK.

At home a fourth float-glass plant was under construction in 1970. Exports of glass reached £18 million in 1969, out of total sales of £48 million from Pilkingtons' British glass plants.

CONCLUSIONS ON DIFFUSION

As a medium-term strategy the Pilkingtons policy of licensing, plus selective overseas investment as a means of maximizing return on their investment in float, has been successful from the company's point of view. It has helped turn a small national concern into an international company – and it has provided resources for further development and growth. Certainly it gave Pilkingtons a surer road to profit and the world's glass manufacturers a more comfortable ride in introducing a major innovation. It could even be argued, though Pilkingtons do not argue this, that the oligopolistic pattern of the world industry and the near monopoly in the home market were a precondition for the huge risk investment which the float process required.

But what happens in the future? Glassmen, like steelmen, like to exert some joint 'control' over their markets, in order to ensure a return on their huge and necessary investments in large plants. So they like 'orderly' pricing, that is to say price leadership and reasonably accepted spheres of market influence. Already, however, within Europe, this approach is breaking down. For Pilkingtons the turning point came when, spurred by the Pilkingtons strike in 1970, its two main vehicle customers, British Leyland and Ford, took clear policy decisions to end their dependence on one supplier and import, in future, a part of their requirements from the Continent. It was not the first time the motor industry had betrayed uneasiness about its reliance on one supplier. From 1950 to 1967 Ford and the British Motor Corporation kept alive a joint subsidiary, British Indestructo Glass (BIG), as an alternative source of supply; that attempt ended in 1967, with the sale of BIG to Triplex, essentially because an enterprise supplying a mere 11·5 per cent of the motor industry's needs (in 1966) was too small to be economic. The fall in tariffs in the Kennedy round, however (from 20 to 10 per cent for motor safety glass imported to the UK), is making importing more attractive. With enlargement of the European Community, the process will go further. Car manufacturers on both sides of the Channel will want to diversify their sources of supply and break the hold which Pilkingtons on one bank and Saint Gobain, Boussois and Glavabel on the other, have on local markets. A new fluidity could give Pilkingtons a chance to increase their market share in Europe and make the policy of licensing (which Saint Gobain has used to good effect by building four float plants) look, in retrospect, rather less wise.

What of the public interest? Licensing diffused the new technology rapidly around the world, but also ensured that the benefits of the new process were brought to the consumer only gradually – that is to say not by rapid price reductions but by a steady fall in real prices over the years.

The Monopolies Commission concluded, after meticulous scrutiny, that Pilkington's monopoly position in the British market was a by-product of excellence, had been a useful base from which they had innovated in the broad national interest, and had not been abused to maintain prices or otherwise exert monopoly power.

In the context of an enlarged European Community, however, the view looks rather different. There the public interest might be still better served if both Pilkingtons and the Continental giants, Saint Gobain, Boussois and Glavabel, penetrate each other's markets more. The motor industry and other users would benefit by being able to turn to a variety of suppliers, competing more effectively on both quality and price. The remnants of the spirit of the 'Sheet-Glass Entente' and the float/plate understanding may have to go.

TWO LICENSEES

From the experiences of the several foreign companies which took licences from Pilkingtons, those of two large American concerns are worth recalling because they throw wider light on the innovation process.

One of the two, call it Company A, took a licence early. A major

90

enterprise with a turnover four times that of Pilkingtons, it had a powerful position in both plate and sheet and strong technological capabilities in fibreglass and chemicals. Yet Company A had difficulty in getting the float process going; there was trouble with materials for lining the furnace and with other parts of the process. Only in the late 1960s, after new drive from the top of the company and changes in personnel, was the process mastered; Company A now has five float plants in operation, a formidable investment.

Company B, on the other hand, had a very different experience. For some time Pilkingtons was reluctant to license this company, which produced mainly for its own needs. Would it obey the rules of an 'orderly' development of the market or would it dump surplus production at disruptive prices? For a year, between 1963 and 1964, Company B spent $1 million of its own funds on building a successful float-glass pilot plant which produced about 50 tons per day. Then, in 1964, Pilkingtons sold it a licence. Alone, Company B would have had to undertake some years of heavy investment to take the float process through to the commercial stage; even then it would have had to pick its way round Pilkington patents. But its own work did give Company B a flying start in taking over and applying what it learnt from Pilkingtons. Company B did this rapidly and has since made a number of improvements to the process which Pilkingtons have used.

Why the difference between the slow application of the process in Company A and the rapid success in Company B? Company A started early, when Pilkingtons themselves were at an earlier stage in the learning process. Company A, too, had very large sums of capital tied up in existing plate and sheet capacity. It had no urgent interest in making these major investments obsolescent until market pressures forced it to put on speed and put a high-quality team on to the float programme.

Two other factors also played a part. As this example illustrates, for a company wanting to make the best use of a licence, it is important to have some knowledge of the technology beforehand. It helps the company to assess how useful the licensed process may be and whether the licensor has found the right answers; if they do have trouble with the process they should have ideas and skills to help in putting it right.

Was the way Company A organized its R and D also a factor which held it back? Process development in Company A is directed from outside the production divisions, in contrast to Pilkington's development groups. Indeed, Company A's major R and D effort is concentrated in its glass research centre, even though the plants have their control laboratories. This is the opposite of Pilkingtons, where glass testing and analysis is done by the central laboratories away from the plants and process development near them. Company A transfers production innovations and ideas from its research centre to the plants by fostering close contacts between the two and encouraging a two-way flow of ideas and information. Communications are also formally organized within three joint committees, composed of research and production people, which meet 'at least every three months' and appoint sub-committees for working follow-ups.

The strength of Company A has been in its mechanized handling, plant control systems and all the other characteristic American methods for getting high productivity out of existing production systems. It is not inappropriate that, in such a system, laboratories for controlling and testing glass production should be attached to the plant.

Pilkingtons' achievement in the 1960s and 1970s has been in radical process innovation. In its case, it has been the development engineers who have been based inside the plant.

CONCLUSION

Pilkingtons, a family business since its foundation 145 years ago, is run by one of Europe's great business families. In other parts of this study we have met family firms which were, like Pilkingtons, prepared to risk long-term investment in technology for the future. The distinction is that Pilkingtons' courage, skill and judgement achieved remarkable success. One feature of this success has certainly been the diverse technical skills of various members of the family and of the management team they have gathered around them; another has been the concentration of the firm's efforts on improving and exploiting its skill in its chosen field, flat glass. Diversification has not diverted it away from making better and better mousetraps.

More than most companies in our study, Pilkingtons has matured smoothly through the crucially difficult transformation from medium-sized firm, based on personal communications, to large public company divisionally organized under modern management methods of control. The strike in 1970, however, which broke a long record of peaceful industrial relations, showed that communications with the shop floor had not kept up with change in other fields. Table 6,

92

Table 6

Giants of World Glass (1969)

	Employment	Turnover (£m)	Profit (£m)	Turnover (£) per man	Profits as % of sales
PPG Industries	40,400	477	22	11,800	4·7
Libby-Owens-Ford	15,959	187	17	11,720	8·9
Asahi	25,065	265	9	10,600	3·4
Saint Gobain	na	436	29	na	2·8
Pilkingtons	30,600	113·4	18·3	3,700	16·1

Note: The companies are listed in probable order of size in flat glass: Asahi and Saint Gobain figures include very large activities outside the flat-glass field. In flat glass Pilkington is comparable in size to Saint Gobain.

comparing the world's leading glass companies, shows that while Pilkingtons had easily the highest rate of profit in 1969 (thanks in part to float), it had easily the lowest turnover per man. In the 1970s three challenges – the need to replace the old paternalistic labour relations and wage structure by a systematic modern industrial relations policy; the withering of the old market-sharing notions in a uniting Europe; and the need to apply the company's brains and resources not just to the glass-making process, but to glass handling and distribution – will put its growing management skills to the test.

93

Chapter 7
SEMICONDUCTORS: INTEGRATION PAYS

'Western European business must act as if a United States of Europe already existed.'

Companies visited:

Texas Instruments (U S A)
S G S (Italy)
Mullards (Philips Group) (U K)
Ferranti (U K)

Integrated circuits were the central innovation in the 1960s in the exploding semiconductor industry. The development of the silicon transistor and then of the tiny integrated circuits, in which a mass of components are grouped on a pin-head-sized clip, has transformed the electronics industry, slashing prices for components as well as their size.

Between January 1970 and January 1971, for instance, prices of three typical products (gates, complex circuits and flip-flops) from a British electronics company fell by between 60 and 76 per cent. In the year 1970 the headlong fall in prices went even faster than usual, but these figures also help to bring home the precipitate improvement brought about by this technological revolution. It is drastically improving the economics of such diverse products as computers, telecommunications equipment and colour television sets.

As the component manufacturers have developed firstly circuits embodying a whole group of components and then large-scale integration in which hundreds of circuits are grouped on a coin-sized chip, their business has invaded that of their customers, the equipment manufacturers, so that the circuit-designer is now intimately involved in the design of the customer's product, while the share of components in the value of products has gone up, despite their tumbling price. By 1969 the US market for semiconductors was worth $1,400 million, compared with $900 million in 1965 and virtually nothing 10 years before; it was expected to grow to $2,000 million by 1975. Starting from scratch in 1962 the market for integrated

94

circuits grew to $85 million in 1965 and some $650 million by 1969. In Europe the market for semiconductors grew from some $300 million in 1965 to some $600 million in 1970 and is expected to grow to about $1,000 million in 1975. The market for integrated circuits has been responsible for a large part of this growth, from $5 million

Table 7

Shares* in the Western European Semiconductor Market (1969)

	Turnover in £ million
Philips Group (Neth.)	44
Texas Instruments (USA)	38
SGS (It.)	18
Siemens (Gy)	17
IT and T (USA)	15
Sescosem (Fr.)	15
Motorola (USA)	12
(Others)	(46)
Total	205

Table 8

Shares in the UK Semiconductor Market (1970)

	Turnover in £ million
Mullard (Philips Group)	13
Texas Instruments	12
Motorola	5
SGS	4
IT and T	4
GEC–EE	3
Ferranti	3
Westinghouse Brake	3
Fairchild	3
Transitron	2
Plessey	2
(Others)	(17)
Total	65

95

in 1965, to \$120 million in 1970 and to an expected \$350–450 million in 1975.

This is an industry where British-owned firms such as Ferranti, our example, had a strong technological position in the early stages. The sheer scale of the American effort, however, plus strong management skills, has since placed them under acute pressure. Low-cost assembly in Asia has tightened the squeeze. In the four cases which follow we compare Texas Instruments (the American world leader), Ferranti and two European enterprises, Philips and SGS, which have tried a multi-national effort to meet the US challenge.

THE RISE OF TEXAS INSTRUMENTS

The US industry first developed through a characteristic mixture of private innovation and exploding government demand. In 1952 the Bell Laboratories expounded the principles of the transistor at a conference for licensees. Texas Instruments, then a small instruments and geophysical exploration firm with a turnover of only \$20 million, took up a licence and embarked privately on a major programme of research, development and investment, which was to average \$4 million in each of the next four years. In 1954 they brought out the first grown-junction silicon transistor, and soon after put germanium transistors into the first transistor radio. Four years later, again using their own resources, they developed the first integrated circuit in the United States.

The integrated circuit revolution was taken a stage further in 1959-60, when Fairchild's semiconductor division (again a smallish enterprise) invented the planar process.

These private developments, however, took place against the background of a formidable growth of government demand and government contracts for R and D. In 1956 the Department of Defense placed major production contracts for transistors (worth some \$30 million). Between 1959 and 1965, US government development contracts for \$100 million were placed for integrated circuits, spurred on by the intense pressure for miniaturization and improved performance which was coming from the missile and space programmes. These contracts came just in time to finance TI's major development programme for ICs. In 1962 the first major government *market* for integrated circuits began to open up, and a contract for 300,000 integrated circuits was placed with TI for the Minuteman Missile programme. In 1965, despite the rapid growth of the civilian market, government contracts were still claiming 75 per cent of the US industry's output of ICs. In 1967, 55 per cent of TI's spending on 'technical effort', or R and D ($100 million), was still supported by government contracts. With the civilian market growing too, as IC applications spilled out firstly into industry and then into consumer products (as the price fell with economies of scale), the US market for integrated circuits was worth some $85 million by 1965.

In integrated circuits TI has been a formidable beneficiary of this explosion of demand, as it has in semiconductors generally. In 15 years it has rocketed up from obscurity to become the world market leader.

TI Turnover

1953	$20 million
1959	$92 million
1969	$832 million
Target for late 1970s	$3 billion

It has not achieved this growth (with one exception) by mergers or acquisitions. The cost of these, in terms of managerial time and effort, is only worth paying, in its view, when there is a very specific and significant increase in technical capability. TI's growth has been internal and is explained by two major factors:

1. *Correct and well-timed technological decisions* taken by a few key people. TI's decision to push ahead with the silicon transistor in 1954 was one of these; the second was the decision, in the late 1950's, to make ICs by the silicon-diffusion process. Westinghouse, which at that time was also a recipient of government R and D funds on a similar large scale, made the wrong decision and tried unsuccessfully to use the money to develop what is called dendritic growth of germanium crystals. Since then TI has continued to take correct technical decisions at the right time – usually backed by government contracts once the decisions have been taken; a recent example is a government contract for the circuitry of a fourth-generation computer composed of a package of large-scale integrated circuits.

2. TI's correct decisions have sprung from their *management philosophy and methods*, the true key to their success; these probably involve the most impressive lessons for Europeans:

(a) The first principle of this philosophy is that the company sets *clear goals* and *works out systematically how to implement them*. OST,

97

almost a company slogan, stands for 'objectives, strategy, tactics'. Long-term goals, or objectives over a period of 5 to 10 years, are set for major areas of the company's business, for instance the Electronics Components Group. These form part of the overall current objective of the company (to expand fivefold within the 10 years to 1975). Within the electronics field particular areas, such as ICs, have more detailed long-term strategies (for turnover, profits, penetration of particular areas of technology or industries and so forth). In still more detail, tactics (or tactical action programmes) provide, for instance, a programme for the development and marketing of a new product together with the attainment of certain turnover and profits targets.

(b) The second feature of the TI system is *systematic delegation of responsibility* for carrying out these aims. The managers of some 70 product/customer centres – for instance, there is one for integrating TTL, one for DTL and linear ICs, one for special integrated circuits, mainly military, and one for advanced circuits – have complete responsibility for achieving the tactical and strategic aims for their products. But though the product/profit centres have much autonomy and power to take decisions over many matters – including purchasing, engineering, production planning and so forth – they are subject to a vigorous monthly reporting system, not only on profits and turnover, but on many other factors also.

(c) *Communication* of the objectives of the company and the methods chosen to achieve them is TI's forte. In a sense the entire system is glorified common sense. What really counts is that everyone in the company appears to know what the system is and what his function is, and is ready to explain it enthusiastically as well.

This successful communication is achieved by minimizing paper and maximizing visual communication and the spoken word. When the entire company structure was modified early in 1968, the managing director of TI's Bedford subsidiary (a profit centre) spent 2 hours briefly explaining personally to everyone (a few minutes with each group of, say, 15) what the changes meant. Blackboard and visual charts are the tools used to expound and mutually criticize monthly achievements of a profit centre.

(d) *Transfer of technology: from development to market.* In a fast-moving technology like integrated circuits, where capital equipment must be written off within 5 years and a product may be obsolete in two, speed in transferring a technological development through production into the market, and in feeding back market requirements into development, is of critical importance. More, perhaps, than any other product, the integrated circuit is an integral part of the design and structure of the user's product; its design is inseparable from the customer's requirements; its technology must be constantly involved with the evolving technology of the user. Texas Instruments has tried to develop systematic means for achieving effective technology transfer, and an effective integration of effort between development and the market. When a new product is developed in the basic semiconductor research laboratory (which serves several product customer centres), the team then moves on to become the nucleus of a technical customer centre (TCC), which operates independently under profit-and-loss criteria but is expected to make a loss in its first years as it takes the new product into production and into the market. Some of the team will stay on as the TCC matures into a fully-fledged product/customer centre (PCC) – a profitable small business in its own right. If the traditional hierarchic company can be described as a pyramid, and even the decentralized product division-based company as a series of small pyramids, TI is better pictured as a complex of mobile cells; new cells are constantly spawned from the fertile ovum of R and D. They are pushed outwards into the commercial world, maturing into small and eventually larger technological businesses, guided only by the basic overall guide lines of OST.

Technology and information transfer in the reverse direction is no less important. In integrated circuits, the seller must increasingly become a consultant to the customer, solving his problems and designing to meet them. Most of TI's salesmen in the IC business are graduate engineers. TI staff are often seconded to work within a customer's operations. Product marketing engineers are of course responsible to TCCs or PCCs.

It need hardly be said, finally, that the vigorous drives of the company's objectives – for rapid growth, especially – impose a dynamic marketing effort. If TI has made some good technical decisions and developments – say for TTL – it has also known how to sell their virtues to customers. And its aggressive marketing policies have included below-cost sales for a calculated period as a means of raising market share to an economic size.

TI and QSEs

In 1971, TI employed some 7,000 QSEs and currently recruits some 1,400 each year; so QSEs made up some 20 per cent of the labour

H

force of 38,700 in 1968. In 1967 it spent about $100 million or 18 per cent of turnover on 'total technical effort'. This figure included more than what is normally described as R and D. Government contracts financed 55 per cent of it. Rather less than half the total was spent in semiconductors.

Its semiconductor laboratory can contain as many as 300 people, say 100 graduates (though it fluctuates as teams are hived off into technical product centres). Total R and D effort in the semiconductor area (including technical product centres) may therefore employ some 500 to 600 people, of whom 250 are graduates.

Texas Instruments has a systematic policy of employee appraisal and development. All employees are assessed annually and promotion and salaries fixed accordingly. A major objective of the company is systematic development of a pool of middle-manager technologists, with a wide experience of the business and a grasp of problems ranging from development to marketing. This aim is served both by individual mobility and by the constant two-way movement of teams between R and D, production and marketing.

Economies of Scale

Leading, as it does, the large US market for ICs and semiconductors, TI has obtained economies of scale in production (as well as development) which few other companies have achieved. In the 1960s only Motorola and TI had fully automated lines for a major part of their IC production right through assembly to computer testing. For very many special products, of course, TI, like other companies, assembles circuits by what seem remarkably primitive methods (pincers under the microscope). But while Fairchild attained its competitive position in the main by assembly in Hong Kong and Seoul (50 cents per day wages), TI has pushed automated production further, though it too is now developing assembly in the Far East.

The Bedford Subsidiary

TI's Bedford subsidiary, employing some 2,000 people and set up only in 1962, benefits from many of the qualities of the parent company. Indeed, while its turnover is not made public, we have reason to believe that output per man was nearly as high as that of the US parent in 1967 (TI Dallas output per man was some £6,300 in 1967 and £7,000 in 1969). How does Bedford achieve this?

One major factor is economies of scale in development. In 1968 TI Bedford was developing only about one-tenth of the products it

100

sold and its R and D laboratory included only some 43 'professionals' (30 graduates). Part of their task was adapting products developed in the USA to production for the British market; but they do some development (in the field of VHF/UHF devices for instance) for the entire TI corporation. Basically, however, TI Bedford relies on the broader R and D effort of the US parent company.

The Bedford enterprise also obtains vital economies of scale by producing only when the market in Britain has reached economic size. Each new product is initially imported to open up the market. Then (in the case of ICs for instance) there may be local assembly, and lastly, when scale warrants it, the diffusion process. A part, but only a part, of their high turnover per man was explained by the relatively substantial level of import content The turnover of TI Bedford may have been about £12 million in 1970; but in terms of locally made products the bulk of this was traditional semi-conductors. Most ICs – and all the latest ones – are still imported. It takes some weeks or months to get a variation of an existing TI product into production in Bedford and up to 18 months to bring in a totally new one (say TTL).

But the most notable feature of the Bedford operation is the extension to it of the parent company's management philosophy. There is the same awareness of company objectives and philosophy and the same classless flavour.

Until the 1970 recession TI Bedford recruited some 20 British graduates each year (for which it had 300 applicants). It was a tribute both to the company's relatively high pay levels (say £2,450 by early 30s) and to the success the company had in selling its image in British universities.

FERRANTI

The Ferranti company is a good deal smaller than Texas Instruments today, but in 1950 it was a larger company. There are nonetheless some parallels between the two.

Like TI, Ferranti was not in semiconductors at all in 1950. In Europe, Mullard and Philips took the lead in germanium components. In October 1953, however, Ferranti put two or three people in a laboratory to work on semiconductor devices. At that stage a first, key, correct technical decision was taken – to go into silicon. The first silicon crystal was pulled in 1954 (i.e. it was about 6 months behind TI).

Ferranti was one of the first in Europe to develop on a commercial

101

scale the epitaxial process for making composite slices of silicon. This made possible transistors with switching characteristics suitable for computers (about November 1959). The planar process led on naturally to integrated circuits.

Ferranti's expansion into semiconductors was, like TI's, helped by its domestic government market, although to a much smaller extent. In particular, work on a computer used to control guided missiles, helped to apply the technology. Integrated circuits required skill in circuit design. Ferranti found that one of the quickest ways to develop a solid state technologist was to take a systems engineer and attach him to semiconductor technology. The semiconductor development was based in part on Ferranti's main computer centre. Internal sales within the company, however, never exceeded 15 per cent of semiconductor turnover.

The problems of scale

Ferranti, however, was of course affected by the huge differences in scale between the USA and Britain in both the public and private market. US demand for ICs in 1969 was worth some $650 million (£270 million) compared with a total British market of £15·4 million (i.e. a factor of 18). In that year the semiconductor market as a whole was put at some £56·5 million in Britain compared with £400 million in the USA. Moreover, Britain in 1969 imported 54 per cent of its public sector requirements for semiconductors. Protection for domestic manufacturers has been more erratic than in the more advanced United States.

The tremendous development of the US market (public and private) had qualitative implications too. Development teams in firms like Texas Instruments had an immense stimulus from a range of highly sophisticated customers; in the defence and space business in the USA there is a market in information – in the form of a wide number of firms, agencies and individuals who meet and communicate information and discuss common problems in a way unknown in Europe. The sheer size of the market, plus the far greater degree of mobility of individuals between firms and government agencies, than in Europe, all help technology transfer and assist the emergence of strong firms.

All this was particularly helpful to a small firm such as Texas Instruments (and it was a small firm in the early 1950s). Its small enthusiastic team could pursue expansion on a single front, achieving growing economies of scale as the firm grew, and feeding on a rich and open market of information and ideas. In a large market, unrestricted by monopoly (though well protected against the outsider), opportunity is there for the small firm. By contrast, Ferranti was operating in a less stimulating technological environment.

Reliance on the smaller unprotected British market meant that Ferranti's turnover in semiconductors has been relatively small. In 1966–67 turnover in integrated circuits was little more than £500,000. By 1970 this had more than doubled but the total semiconductor turnover was only some £3·5 million (equivalent to 4 per cent of the market of all Western Europe).

This modest size clearly had an impact on the scale of research and development. In the years 1958–61, Ferranti's semiconductor business, though small, was highly profitable. Development could take as much as a fifth of expenditure. This was the era of high-cost, small-scale production before the planar era. In the 1960s, thanks to the huge expansion of the American market and of American output, there took place a dramatic fall in market prices in semiconductors. At the same time the minimum scale necessary to successful development is growing rapidly.

In 1969 Ferranti spent £311,000 on R and D in micro-circuits, just over 20 per cent of turnover. But for integrated circuits alone it now ought, on its own estimates, to be spending at least some £600,000 per year, and most people would regard £1 million, or almost as much as Ferranti's integrated circuit sales, as the barest minimum, and probably far below it.

Ferranti's R and D team in semiconductors consisted of some 45 graduates and 18 with other QSE qualifications. Texas Instruments, by comparison, employed some 250 graduates in semiconductor R and D. Through the sheer scale of the American market and effort in semiconductors, a technological gap, in the precise sense of the work, still exists in this industry. Ferranti, it will be recalled, was perhaps a year behind TI in 1953–54 when the two were entering the semiconductor business. Today it is still behind by a similar period of time. By mid-1970 Ferranti had not yet seriously entered the field of large-scale integration – the massing of up to a thousand circuits on a single chip – in which TI leads. Thanks to the concentration of brains and capability, America is still the hub of world development in integrated circuits.

In competition with US firms, European companies have on their side the mitigating factor that American subsidiaries, though in theory they can import a product as soon as it is introduced in the

103

USA, in practice take 6–18 months to introduce it into production here. Other things being equal, European companies naturally also prefer service and technical dialogue with companies who develop and produce on the spot. For a European supplier of ICs, therefore, a few months' 'gap' presents no insuperable difficulties. All the same, if European companies are to command a major sector of the European market, they cannot remain essentially followers of a technology originating in the USA. And that brings us back to the scale of effort in research and development.

In production, too, firms in the United States can achieve some economies of scale that are unobtainable in Europe; European enterprises may achieve a degree of automation comparable to US firms on individual, long, production runs, but the scale of the more homogeneous US market means that a larger proportion of their business is in such long and economic runs.

Divisions in the European Market

At present the European market is divided by the following factors:

(1) Since defence and government demands are smaller, a far larger proportion of the European market than in America in the 1970s will be for consumer products, which tends to mean a much greater variety of demands. The relatively larger number and smaller size of European companies also breaks up the market.

(2) Varying national standards, plus economic nationalism, also inhibit sales of integrated circuits from one economic production point to the entire European market. Anxious as they are to have some kind of local production capability in this key product, which penetrates so many other industries, Britain, France and, increasingly, Germany, all place pressure on manufacturers to assemble and even diffuse integrated circuits within their national frontiers. For a firm such as Ferranti which at present has a negligible share of markets outside the home country, this would mean not only developing a sales network but investing in assembly and ultimately separate diffusion facilities. It has made a start in one other major national market, but quite clearly a very large investment is needed to transform what is basically a national marketing network into a European one. Separate diffusion and assembly facilities also mean higher costs in over-heads, and in uneconomic use of plant. And though US companies meet the same problems in Europe, they start with the advantage

104

of concentrated production facilities at home where they can make those circuits for which there are large economies of scale.

For a European company to achieve efficient operation evidently means serving the European market as a whole. That, in turn, places a premium on marketing ability and transfer of technology within the enterprise between development and the market.

SGS: GROWING UP WITH FAIRCHILD

In the 1960s Italy's Società Generale Semiconduttori was one of Europe's most interesting advanced-technology enterprises. Set up in 1957, it grew in less than 10 years to become what was claimed to be the largest non-American manufacturer of silicon planar semiconductors, with a turnover of over $40 million in 1969. Five features of its story stand out:

(1) The enterprise began by uninhibited partnership with a major US company from which it rapidly acquired skill in a new advanced technology.
(2) Though this US company had a holding in SGS, it was always a minority holding. When, as often happens, the interests of the partners began to diverge, the Italian partners were able to buy the US partners out.
(3) During the crucial formative years when SGS was building on Fairchild technology its top priority was to develop a powerful marketing network throughout Europe. Marketing came first and when its own development effort built up it fed into a market-oriented concern.
(4) In the years 1964 to 1970, SGS's management structure acquired a co-operative European flavour which made it a social innovator in this industry. To quote the company: 'SGS has pioneered the concept that Western European business must act as if a United States of Europe already existed.'
(5) In response to the squeeze on profits and prices in 1970, however, it reverted to a more traditional centralized management structure.

As a story of acquiring and building on US technology the tale of SGS has an almost Japanese flavour.

Phase I: Germanium Semiconductors
SGS was set up in the 1950s by Olivetti and Telettra on a 50–50 basis,

105

to produce germanium transistors and diodes under a licence agreement with General Electric. Its main markets at first were the two parent companies.

Phase II: Partnership with Fairchild

Meanwhile, in the USA, the scientists who invented the planar transistor looked about for a US company to back them, but found all except Fairchild committed to other processes. Fairchild Camera, however, formed a wholly owned division, Fairchild semiconductors, to exploit the process.

Coming late into the market, it had its work cut out getting a foothold in the United States. At first its main sales line was reliability and its main market military. The small scale of production kept costs high; with its hands full in the United States, Fairchild sought partners to help it into Europe.

In Europe, the SGS management had realized the significance of the planar transistor and quickly decided to get in touch with Fairchild. The common interest was evident. Fairchild offered them sole rights in planar transistors in Europe, Africa and the Middle East if they would set up a Europe-wide marketing network. SGS accepted and, when its licence with GE expired, sold its germanium equipment to a Yugoslavian company.

Fairchild acquired one-third of the shares from Olivetti and Telettra, so that each partner would now hold one-third of the shares.

Marketing outlets were then developed in Germany, France, Sweden and the UK. Application laboratories were set up, first in Italy and then in Germany, France and Britain. At first, demand was supplied mainly from the USA, but manufacturing capacity was built up fast between 1961 and 1964. Olivetti is a company with a strong sense of the need for individual participation and for close contact between workers and the top. It became company policy to develop a manufacturing plant in each major country, 80 per cent self-sufficient and close to market needs. In Britain for instance, the new Falkirk production facility was employing 1,200 people by 1969.

Research and Development

In 1966 SGS decided to develop their own basic R and D:

(a) to make possible more rapid transfer of US knowhow to Europe; and

(b) to develop products suitable for the European market (e.g. transistors and integrated circuits for the entertainment industry), whose requirements are often different from those of the USA.

The aim was to do R and D which was complementary to Fairchild's. By 1968 the R and D effort was equivalent to 5 per cent of a turnover of £12·5 million, or some £600,000 per year. SGS had 80 QSES on R and D, plus back-up, in other words an effort very similar in scale to Ferranti's. Output per man (and woman) in 1968 was some £3,700 per head for a labour force of 3,400. Even at this stage, however, the R and D effort did not compare in scale with the marketing effort, in terms of numbers of QSES employed. SGS cannot afford to be reluctant about marketing for its very existence depends on selling throughout Europe to the commercial market. It had over three times as many qualified people (say ONC and over) in marketing (300) as in R and D (80) and over twice as many graduates (70–30). It was a notable contrast with another British company in the same field, which was employing about the same number of QSES in R and D but less than 30 in marketing.

The Italian market is far less developed than, say, the British and there is very little government business, so SGS sells on about an equal scale to the four major European markets. Its turnover of some 9 per cent of the European semiconductor market in 1969 was spread throughout Europe. Its share of the European IC market was rather larger. Together with Philips (producing in Germany, France, Holland, UK) and TI (UK, France, Germany), it was one of the three semiconductor companies to produce throughout Europe; all others are national. SGS had both diffusion and assembly facilities in the UK and France, as well as Italy, and assembles in Germany and Sweden too.

At the time of the break with Fairchild, SGS was faced with the problems of the *division of the European market* in a big way. It had, mainly as a legacy from Fairchild, to satisfy some 20,000 different semiconductor specifications (not quite as difficult as it seems as these were derived mainly from selection of finished products). Also as a legacy, it produced essentially by primitive tweezer and microscope methods. It carried extra cost in overheads (five production centres, plus extra communication cost, etc.), wafer fabrication and, to some degree, assembly. Local test facilities and applications engineering near the customer made economic sense; the rest did not and derived essentially from economic nationalism.

Phase III: The Break with Fairchild

Until 1969, sgs overcame some of the problems of *scale in develop-ment* by its link with Fairchild. Its management were fully aware that alone they could not possibly cross the minimum threshold of development and keep in the front rank, for instance, in the new expensive phase of large-scale integration. Drawing on Fairchild's R and D effort (some 600 graduates strong) was basic to the business. Both companies kept resident engineers in each other's enterprise. New products were at first bought from Fairchild, but could be made by sgs within 6 months. Technology transfer seemed to an observer to be quite as good as in ti, and Fairchild made no attempt to dominate or interfere.

As sgs applications laboratories built up, however, employing many research people who had been to Fairchild in the usa, it gradually developed an independent team, doing work not done in the usa.

Fairchild's us work was mostly fallout from the space programme, producing expensive products unsuitable for Europe. Even in the domestic fields, American tv is so different that design engineers in Europe using us devices must compensate in their circuit designs. A difference of objective between Fairchild and sgs began to appear, with Fairchild wanting to maximize exports and doubtful of sgs's growing production and R and D.

In 1968 Fairchild's attempt to take sgs over was rebuffed by Olivetti and Telettra. At the time Fairchild was in difficulties at home. So it sold out its holding, leaving the Italian partners a free hand. Olivetti afterwards took over the remaining Telettra sharehold-ing, acquiring complete control.

sgs is now free to trade worldwide (before it was limited to Europe, the Middle East and Africa). Following the example of American semiconductor manufacturers, who seek cheap labour for assembly work in the Far East, it has opened a new factory in Singapore which will employ 3,000 people and open a door to the us and Asian markets.

sgs formed a mechanization department in its R and D labora-tories in late 1968, charged with the job of automating production whenever possible and increasing output per worker. New production techniques devised by this body were gradually introduced into sgs factories during late 1969 and early 1970 and considerably raised the group's economic production threshold. To take advantage of this and of the slackening of the economic nationalism in Europe, in mid-1970 the requirement that each national company be 80 per cent self-sufficient in its production was scrapped. An international production planning department was formed, with staff from each company serving on it, and production was divided by product lines between the various factories to obtain the maximum production runs, usually on the basis of where a particular technology was most easily implemented. All this was achieved without taking away the essential autonomy and national motivation of each company. Its main human effect was to give each general manager a few extra 'ground rules' to adhere to in international executive committee meetings. Production control was handled by computer in the international department.

Research and Development

With the Fairchild links severed, SGS was obliged to expand its own R and D effort rapidly. By 1970 SGS was employing some 400 QSES on R and D, and spending some 12 per cent of turnover on it (say £2 million).

SGS evolved a new family of high-level logic ICs unique in the world for noise immunity, and the first effective world replacement for electro-mechanical relays and switches. In addition it developed a completely new system of diffusing MOS devices, overcoming the greatest disadvantage of these by a unique process (now called Planox) whereby a flat surface is achieved on the device, making it extremely reliable. In at least six areas of silicon technology SGS claimed its research was ahead of the Americans'. The problem of scale, however, remains pressing. And up till 1970 SGS was willing to find solutions by co-operating with other Europeans.

Technology Transfer: a Co-operative Structure

All the evidence was that SGS encountered few problems in the 1960s in transferring technology between market and development. At first this was because the firm was small and market-oriented. Development engineers visited customers; in Italy a product marketing committee and a product planning committee worked intimately together. Two formal features of company organization helped the process on:

1. In each of the major national enterprises there was a device engineering laboratory. These laboratories were responsible to their

109

international general manager for all their company's custom (bespoke) integrated circuit design activity and design of proprietary (standard) devices on technologies developed by the central R and D laboratories. They were also responsible for product transfer from development to production.

The scientist who developed a product went with it and worked with the production engineer who had to put it into production. Transfer from R and D into production took about 6 months.

2. Until 1970 the company as a whole had a two-tier international management structure which both facilitated communication and illustrated the company's ethics – that of a European team.

Each of SGS's 6 companies had a general manager; all were members of the international executive committee together with the international director of R and D, the international director of operations, the international director of finance, the international director of personnel, the international director of planning and the international managing director. This committee made group policy, under the wing of the board.

The functional international managers listed above acted as communicators, ensuring that those with similar functions in the various companies communicated together. Another job of the international managers was to scour the world for new ideas, bringing them to the attention of line managers in each company; they also stopped duplication by communicating and making sure that each company knew what others were doing.

Phase IV: Retrenchment and Central Control
In 1970 the squeeze on prices and profits hit SGS, as it did other European semiconductor manufacturers. It forced the company to retrench. It abandoned the co-operative management structure developed in the previous years, closed down production facilities in Germany and Sweden, placed national marketing organizations directly under an Italian functional director, and did the same with its remaining production facilities (for instance in Scotland) outside Italy. It closed down its application laboratories outside Italy. In April 1971 it announced an agreement with Motorola to double-source some of the two companies' integrated circuit products in Europe. That is to say, when one of the partners is unable to supply a particular product, it automatically draws on the other. Later in 1971 Olivetti sold out the bulk of its holding to IRI, the Italian state-

holding enterprise. STET, IRI's telecommunications group, brought SGS together with ATES, a smaller STET electronic components enterprise. STET now holds 60 per cent of the shares of the new combined company, Olivetti 20 per cent and Fiat 20 per cent.

Conclusion

Market orientation was SGS's main virtue in the 1960s. Like Texas Instruments, SGS maintained the impetus for innovation by giving relatively small profit centres wide autonomy. Many writers on innovation have stressed that it flourishes not within a hierarchic organization, but in a mobile cellular structure where small co-operative groups, freely communicating with each other, are in a position to initiate change. This was the formula in SGS between 1968 and 1970. But the reversion to a classic centralized national control, a response to a short-term cash flow problem, has changed the picture.

How have the company's results reflected its success in building a Europe-wide enterprise on the basis of American technology and market-orientation?

Turnover of the company, £12·4 million in 1967/8, was over £17 million by 1969. Before 1970 SGS was profitable, but did not disclose figures to us. The crash in prices, however, evidently plunged the company into the red. Lacking the resources of a wider group (which Philips had) or the government market (which US companies still have), even a company of SGS's size was not able to remain in the gruelling semiconductor race. IRI's backing now gives it a more solid base.

Its vulnerability means that, despite its rapid growth, SGS might still be open to some form of combination with other European enterprises as a means of growing even faster.

One possible solution might be a joint co-operative agreement between major European manufacturers on R and D. This could be in such fields as the development of software for computer-aided design, where no commercial secrets are involved and present duplication of effort is wasteful. Different manufacturers could allocate development of logical families between them, to save resources and rationalize the work. Every experiment in European technological collaboration so far has, however, shown that common R and D without common production and marketing, can come unstuck. The best way to avoid this danger is to merge in some way.

Outside the giant conglomerates, Philips and Siemens, which will almost certainly want to retain their semiconductor capabilities in the firm, SGS, COSEM in France and Ferranti and Plessey in Britain, all offer potential ingredients for a stronger European enterprise.

MULLARD-PHILIPS

The Mullard company, Philips' electronic component enterprise in Britain, is Britain's largest manufacturer of semiconductors (with a turnover of, say, £12 to £15 million – 20 per cent of the market – in 1970), just ahead of Texas Instruments. It came, however, late into the integrated circuit business, making only some £300,000 worth in 1967. Like some large American companies, Philips, Europe's largest electrical company, failed to appreciate the silicon revolution in 1952 and was slow again to recognize the significance of Fairchild's planar diffusion process (1960). Philips Eindhoven are a highly consumer-oriented company and were therefore attached to germanium. They cleverly invented alloy-diffused transistors in the 1950s, which attached them further to germanium, and did not appreciate the cheapness and facility with which silicon can be diffused to form a layer. When ICs came on the market it was thought they were suitable for digital, not consumer, applications – Philips' main in-house need; so there was further delay. In Philips, in short, both silicon and integrated circuits came up against the well-known, big-company syndrome, 'not invented here'.

In 1959, however, Mullard and Philips at last got into the silicon component business, 5 years behind Ferranti, and started off in integrated circuits in 1965. The late start was plainly a handicap. But it is at this point that the advantages of size and of Philips' Europe-wide character and operations become clear. Let us, briefly, look at these.

The Philips Philosophy: a Paradoxical Balance between Independence and Unity

A basic principle of Philips is the independence of the hierarchies based (a) on nationality and geography, and (b) on main industrial group activities. Philips is, in a sense, a confederation of autonomous empires, for in the historical period in which it has grown up it had to live with European nationalism. The company's philosophy has been that independence is necessary if companies are to thrive within a national environment, or indeed develop an impetus and dynamism of their own. National colouring is necessary to win governments' acceptance. Yet, at the same time, member companies

112

ought to be able to draw on the research and marketing capability of the entire empire. Philips thus blends a degree of nationalism with universality. It is a notable contrast with the uniformity of doctrine in such American newcomers as TI, but not with older-established, federal-type US companies in Europe like IT and T.

The Structure

In the major industrial countries, Philips is divided in main industry groups (11 in all). In the UK these are then grouped in three major divisions: consumer goods (Philips Electrical), electronic and capital goods, and components (Mullard).

These three divisions are highly independent of each other. One major reason is that many customers of Mullard (say) for components (e.g. TV tubes or integrated circuits) may be competitors of other Philips companies in finished products. All decisions on capital investment up to, say, seven figures, are taken by the Mullard board, a notable mark of independence.

Yet Philips companies also benefit from their ability to pool resources internationally. There are voluntary agreements to specialize on particular products in particular countries, for instance in consumer goods. There is also some rationalization of design and manufacturing methods, i.e. techniques for manufacturing a product learnt in one country are used in another. An engineer with a problem may telephone or visit a laboratory or manufacturing unit elsewhere in the company which has experience in the same field.

Common yardsticks of efficiency are disseminated, e.g. there is a quarterly comparison of yield on integrated circuits in all European plants, an important yardstick for the engineer.

The supplier of semiconductors can call on an alternative source of supply in another country if production breaks down or cannot meet demand.

In research, and in finance, Philips' confederal structure is also apparent. Their research laboratory at Eindhoven, employing some 2,400 people (400 of them Ph.D.-level QSES), serves the whole company, but all major countries also have a major applied research laboratory, to make possible contact with local customers, meet defence needs, and so on. In Britain the main laboratory, which does essentially applied research, is at Salfords, Surrey, and is part of the Mullard company, for which it does 80 per cent of its work. In semiconductors the heart of the Mullard industrial R and D work is at Southampton (120 QSES), next to the main semiconductor plant.

As for finance, Philips, like TI, has a detailed monthly system of reporting on turnover, profits, costs and a great many other details. The leaders of this vast and scattered empire which has, after all, been growing steadily since the 1880s, aim not, like TI, at a ruthless and furious expansion but rather at holding their own comfortably and advancing at a steady jog trot.

Nonetheless, when they choose to make a determined effort to catch up (as Philips/Mullard are doing in ICs) or push ahead, they can bring to bear massive resources and draw on a formidable reservoir of inventive skills. Work on ICs is now being pushed fast, not only at Eindhoven, but in at least 4 national laboratories (UK, France, Holland, Germany) with Mullard playing a leading part. In development, Mullard is now pushing ahead with large-scale integration and is now only a short head behind Texas Instruments.

Mullard, and its sister Philips companies (unlike Ferranti), also benefit from some economies of scale within the European market, since they are able to operate a certain division of labour in research, development, and production and to draw continuously on a common pool of knowledge.

Agreement, for instance, has been reached between the four European Philips enterprises on standardized production processes for ICs. Identical IC masks are made in each country when the needs are the same, making transfer easy to fill orders or production gaps.

Philips (mistakenly perhaps) lower their productivity by servicing the whole market, to please their huge range of customers. This TI does not do. But Philips do achieve some economies of scale by specialized development and production; TTL is made in the UK, Suhl 1 and 2 in France, DTL in Holland and linear development for the consumer market in Germany. In research, gallium phosphide work is concentrated in Germany, gallium arsenide in Salfords, and so on. Given the divisions and variety of the European market, Philips, with its subtle confederal structure, is probably better placed to overcome them and achieve some kind of economies of scale than any other company.

Policy on QSEs: Research and Market

Mullard, like Ferranti and TI, is an engineer-led company. Of the 7 executive directors, 5 are QSEs; perhaps 1,000 of the 17,000 labour force are QSEs (say 6 per cent), of which some 700 are scientific and technical graduates. QSEs are paid on rates roughly equivalent to those in the scientific civil service; there are also generous fringe benefits (e.g. up to 12 month's sick pay).

Mullard does not, it seems, suffer from any particular gap between R and D and the market. Customer interest is one factor in deciding research work, together with the international pressures (regular meetings of the heads of Philips laboratories etc.) and others. Marketing and attitudes to the market are said to be improving; but the wrong decisions taken in the 1950s on semiconductors illustrate a characteristic Philips weakness: the tendency to produce products for a market determined by their own internal needs.

Conclusion: Philips

The Philips giant made a late start in the silicon revolution, as it did in computers. Massive investment, however, enabled it to catch up and hold its place as Europe's leading semiconductor manufacturer. Co-operation and a division of labour between its enterprises in different countries go some way toward giving it economies of scale comparable to those attainable by companies in the United States.

CONCLUSION: SEMICONDUCTORS AND INTEGRATED CIRCUITS

The semiconductor industry is one where a huge scale is needed in R and D and where, therefore, the size of the American market and of US government support have helped generate American industrial leadership and a classic 'technological' gap. Yet European-owned industry should not lose hope. Here, as in so many other fields, the Western European market is growing faster than the American; moreover, if it is smaller and weaker in terms of sophisticated defence equipment and capital goods, the market for consumer products is relatively larger. At the industrial level Philips, despite a late start in silicon, has shown that it is possible to retain a strong position, by massive and continuous investment and a systematic effort to pool development and production resources throughout Europe.

Just how difficult this is has been shown, however, by the examples of SGS and Ferranti. When recession hit the industry in 1970, Philips, as on other occasions, was able to absorb the financial shock without seriously impairing its strategic plans. SGS made a more ruthless cutback which could harm its future prospects and has checked its attempt to build up an enterprise of European style. None of the remaining British-based semiconductor and IC enterprises (GEC,

Plessey, Ferranti) appear to have the scale for long-term viability. Companies of their scale and character and perhaps even that of sgs may need to merge with partners to achieve long-term strength and stability.

This process will not be helped in Europe by protectionist measures at national level. They split the European market further and do nothing to awaken the marketing capability which some European companies lack.

But three positive government actions could be helpful to get at the roots of the problem in integrated circuits: the divided European market. One is to push ahead with the development and real application of common European standards in the public sector. Government, above all the Post Office, provides about half the British market for integrated circuits. By 1975 the Post Office could be absorbing £35 million worth of ICs. It is high time it put into practice the Burghard standards agreed on a European scale. Each of the major British government users at present has a separate inspection department. Full adoption of the new standard would make possible an amalgamation of these inspection departments. The numbers of inspectors could be cut by several thousand making possible a big saving in public funds.

The second evident field for action by European governments is the effective creation of a common public market for this key industry.

In development, a strong integrated circuit industry will not be created just by subsidies. But it might be stimulated by major European development projects, with clear goals. At the European level, for instance, major joint communications system developments might be made the instrument of more advanced component development within European standards, and on a basis of co-operation.

In two other cases in this study (nuclear power, and variable geometry aircraft) government support has been critical to the first important steps toward a European industry. In semiconductors, too, it seems unlikely that major steps will be made to pull together some of the fragmented European industry unless governments take decisions of principle to support the industry at a European level, or at least give specific encouragement to cross-frontier mergers between companies such as sgs and Sescosem and the semiconductor activities of UK companies such as GEC, Plessey and Ferranti.

Even if European companies of this kind do emerge, they will not succeed unless they can achieve some of the market orientation and managerial skill so evident in Texas Instruments. François Giroud

116

recently summarized the reasons for Japan's current economic performance as: *'Le génie qu'il faut.'*

In Texas Instruments, too, there is something of that carefully disciplined creative energy which makes for success in transforming technology from invention into the market place.

Chapter 8
THE BIRTH OF COLOUR TELEVISION:
A CASE OF SIZE

Companies visited:

EMI (UK)
Marconi (USA)
RCA (USA)

The pioneering of monochrome television in the 1930s by EMI and RCA was one of the classics of competitive innovation, prewar-style. Working with a team of some 30 QSEs, led by the remarkable Schonberg, EMI put the world's first commercial television into service from Alexandra Palace in 1936.

By the time colour television appeared after the war the scene had changed completely. RCA's NTSC system provided the basis for the world's colour television development, and for the British Post Office the major decision in the 1960s was whether to adopt the German PAL or French SECAM variations on it. How did this shift in the balance of technological leadership take place and what did it imply?

Ever since the 1920s the companies concerned have shared a great deal of knowledge and have often been linked by formal agreements to exchange knowhow and patents. Before the war, the two companies RCA and EMI worked in parallel; each knew of and benefited from the work of the other in the framework of an agreement on the exchange of patents and knowhow; the technology was fundamentally similar, though differing in some respects, such as the number of lines and frame rate. This last difference was partly due to the difference in power supply frequency employed in the USA and Europe.

First into the field with an all-electronic black and white television system, EMI had the disadvantages as well as advantages of leadership. It proposed a 405-line system. By the time RCA came into the market, the technology had advanced sufficiently far to allow a 525-line system. RCA also had the benefit of experience gained in Britain to set further parameters on the transmission system, including negative modulation and the use of frequency modulation sound. The other Europeans coming in still later, were able to start off with 625 lines.

In the same way (though in reverse) the Europeans were later able to improve on the colour television system introduced first by RCA.

The war gave a tremendous boost to the electronics industry on both sides of the Atlantic and indeed precipitated key technological advances (wide-band transmission, high-frequency measuring instruments) which were essential to colour television. But it also left the environment and relative position of the companies completely changed. Before the war, the companies concerned had something like a monopoly of knowhow in the field. And EMI had, if anything, benefited from the existence of a national public broadcasting system which had been bolder in taking the initiative in sponsoring television services than private US sponsors. During the war the British electronics industry became part of a remarkable national effort in which teams of individuals from industry, universities and Government were fused together and information was fully shared. But when the war ended and the psychological barriers between government laboratories and private industry reappeared, prewar teams had sometimes been broken up; the firms that had been most closely involved with the Government were not necessarily those best placed in the commercial field.

In the USA, by contrast, most wartime electronics development took place in private industry, and RCA, whose expenditure (of $9 million) in the 1930s had been no larger than EMI's (£2–3 million), emerged into the postwar period with the financial and technical strength to make the establishment of a colour television system a credible goal for the company's president, David Sarnoff, in 1945.

The contrast between the position of the companies was matched by a difference in postwar national environment. In austere Britain the BBC had its work cut out getting a monochrome TV system established, and it gave no encouragement to British companies to develop a colour system. In postwar America incomes were high enough to appear to offer a big and early market for colour television.

Even so RCA would not have pushed ahead with colour development so fast but for a competitive challenge. RCA's own monochrome television system had just reached the commercial stage in 1947 when the rival broadcasting network, CBS, produced a mechanical colour system and persuaded the Federal Communications Commission to recommend an immediate jump to colour using the CBS system. RCA was convinced from the start that a system of this kind, which was not compatible with an electronic monochrome system, was impractical, but it was obliged to mount both a crash programme of development for a compatible colour system and a formidable lobbying campaign to win its point.

119

By 1951 it had overcome the main technical problems and was winning the support of the National Television Systems Committee set up by US industry. Through this committee the RCA system benefited from contributions from other US companies, such as the Haseltine Corporation. RCA in turn, in accordance with its policy of licensing its patents to others, supplied information to competing tube manufacturers on its tri-colour kinescope tube. In 1953, after a series of hearings and tests performed by the FCC, the FCC accepted the RCA (or NTSC) system.

RCA had, by now, done all the development and engineering work on the system; in October 1953 it turned over freely to engineers representing TV set manufacturers, full details of the design and performance of the RCA colour TV receiver. It did this because it took the view that a totally new market of this kind could not be developed by one manufacturer alone. RCA's major subsidiary, the National Broadcasting Corporation (NBC), was now in a position to start broadcasting in colour, but several years were required to develop the market; it became significant about 1961–62 and reached five million sets in 1966.

The smaller British companies, EMI and Marconi, faced no such challenge to develop a colour system as RCA did from CBS and the FCC in the late 1940s. And when they faced the problem in the early 1950s they decided, rightly or wrongly, that colour television, a great deal more sophisticated than monochrome in its techniques, was too expensive to tackle alone. The cost of developing the full range of equipment needed has been estimated to us as between 5 and 15 times the cost of monochrome, that is between $30 million and $90 million depending on when you started and on how quickly you tried to do it. EMI's total turnover in 1950 was only £30 million (or about what RCA had to spend on the development).

The decision not to go it alone was helped by the existence since the war of a strong tradition of cross-licensing and knowhow exchange in the world electronics industry and, in particular, by the unique position of RCA. RCA, originally a subsidiary of Marconi set up during the First World War, was hived off to become an independent corporation under the encouragement of the US Government. It has a company policy of licensing its patents to others, including European manufacturers, as well as a long historical association with Marconi. EMI's prewar knowhow agreement with RCA lapsed after the war, but it continued to have a patent agreement with RCA and later with Telefunken.

120

Marconi started work on colour TV some 2 or 3 years later than RCA in their research laboratories and by 1952 they had an idea of the type of system they could develop, although they were not as far ahead as RCA were in 1951 and had spent only £1 million ($2·8 million) compared with RCA's spending of about $15–20 million; at that stage they abandoned work on an independent system, both because they lacked resources and because they had no business in commercial receivers, as RCA did.

EMI pursued a rather similar course with rather fewer QSEs (3 or 4, compared with 9 or 10) and got to a similar position about a year later. They did some work on the Colombia system and realized that RCA's was best. They felt that the BBC, concerned for world compatibility, would not encourage the development of a system different from RCA's. They knew that in any case they did not have the resources. Both Marconi and EMI subsequently concentrated on the camera side of the business, and on other studio equipment (vision mixers, control circuitry and so on) in the case of EMI; Marconi began by building colour cameras to RCA licence (in small numbers) during the 1950s, and then developed their own cameras fast when they thought the UK market was ready and the US market ripe for an attack, which happened to be in 1965/6.

By 1969 both EMI and Marconi were selling cameras quite successfully in the UK market (about 60–100 each); Marconi had also sold to the USA (maybe 100) and EMI to France (number not known). Their penetration of these markets has undoubtedly been assisted by the use of the Philips Plumbicon tube, whereas RCA originally used image orthicon tubes, then videcon tubes, and only later the more sensitive and more complex Plumbicon. When RCA designed its camera the Plumbicon was not available, and if the other two had developed their cameras before about 1964 they would have missed it too. But their cameras also embody excellent features developed by EMI and Marconi, or so it would appear because the Marconi camera sold at $80,000 in the US in 1968, compared to the Philips ($60,000) and RCA ($70,000) models.

THE COMPANIES APPRAISED

Obviously, RCA is the real leader in this field; Telefunken and CSF have usefully improved the NTSC system (with the PAL and SECAM systems). Thus PAL has stabilized the transmission signal – at some cost, but bringing greater reliability and ease of operation. Both

121

systems are, however, only important variations on NTSC (the RCA system) and not major alternatives.

Similarly, Marconi and EMI are not producers of a full system and can expect only very modest overall sales figures in cameras compared to those obtainable for a complete range of domestic receivers, transmitters and cameras. (Strictly speaking, one should exclude transmitters from this field since they are a field on their own, and are little different from monochrome transmitters.)

But although RCA are the leaders (the American sales of receivers by all companies may have totalled $7–8 billion by the end of 1968), they had to carry a long period of market development after 1955, as well as the ten or more years of large-scale investment in R and D, before their massive innovation paid off. This difficult phase was reflected in the price of RCA shares at the time. Once the market had been developed in the USA, it was considerably easier to develop it in Europe.

Marconi and EMI have so far made a success out of the sector of the market they entered. They had sold 150–200 cameras each at about $20,000 per camera by 1969, a revenue of £3–4 million on an investment of £350,000 to £450,000 each. After only 2 years they had sold equipment to a value of ten times the R and D cost, and in a 10-year period they might expect to sell five times as much – £15–20 million (these are our rough guesses) – against a limited continuing development expenditure in improvements to the product.

Marconi's and EMI's effort in the field of colour TV is, nevertheless, not comparable to that of RCA, because they made little attempt to develop a full system, and that only up to about 1952 when the hard part of the task would have begun if they had continued. Furthermore, although each of them has developed independently its major colour TV product, the camera, Marconi benefited to a considerable degree from technology transfer from RCA. Marconi built a camera under licence from RCA during the 1950s and had only a minimal stake in the technology at that time. The serious effort of both companies was sustained for a much shorter period (3 to 5 years in the early 1960s); previously they were not playing an innovative role in colour TV.

CONTRASTS BETWEEN THE COMPANIES: THE BRITISH
COMPANIES HAVE NO CONSUMER INTERESTS

Both the US and the British electronics industries developed at a phenomenal rate during the Second World War, and many of

122

the colour TV techniques became possible as a result of work in that period. But a basic difference between the industries is obvious with very little examination. In Britain, as a result of changes in structure during the 1930s and 1950s, there are a number of companies which deal primarily with the consumer market and another group which handles capital equipment. In the USA, on the other hand, the largest manufacturers of capital goods also supply the domestic market with consumer equipment. The three companies studied are no exception to this generalization, although EMI is rather an unusual example. RCA is a large, diversified but largely electronics company which has grown up with the business in almost all fields. Marconi is very much a technically oriented company, which has always (apart from a decadent spell as part of Cable and Wireless) been at the forefront of technology (radio, valves, radar), but it has usually shed an activity which looked like being too competitive commercially. In the past it might have been suggested, with no element of criticism, that it represented the company which is technologically motivated and does not succeed in making (or perhaps even attempt to make) technology very profitable commercially. Thus it sought research contracts from the Government and organized its production facilities as general purpose workshops for batch production of high-skill contracts work. Its main foothold in commercial fields is on broadcasting equipment, where again the competitive edge is technical and not commercial. EMI is an unusual example of the British electronic capital goods manufacturer. Before the war it made radios, records and gramophones, and the world's first operating TV system came from the company. But though it got rid of the consumer electronics business in the mid-1950s, its attempts to develop new capital goods – computers, NC for machine tools, radar, etc. – were frequently unsuccessful, more through a lack of commercial orientation than through poor technology; its bread and butter was the very profitable gramophone record business.

We found it hard to pin down just where EMI's management went wrong. Perhaps there was a classic British gulf between a dynamic, commercially oriented, entertainments business and technologists interested in technology for technology's sake. When we visited EMI technologists no longer had the authority on the board which, for instance, Schonberg had; but changes have been made more recently.

An important shift in structure is now taking place at EMI. Entertainments, the record companies and electronics are each being grouped in a separate division. The small managing board for electronics will consist of a chief executive and directors for finance, commercial matters and R and D. Success in the future may well depend on whether, in setting strategic objectives, a real synthesis can be achieved between technological potential and commercial ends.

All three companies are now remarkably similar in their basic R and D organization structure. They have central laboratories doing the purer research and development laboratories attached each one to a product division.

RCA was the first to establish this pattern. In the 1930s it had a centralized research facility devoted to broad new electronic fields; the product/profit centres also carried out advanced development work appropriate to their interests. During the 1940s, RCA strengthened its central facilities and undertook more basic research. The product divisions continued to carry out advanced development and undertook some research work under grants from the central research laboratory. Some of the product divisions also established development functions at the central research facility, to help technology transfer. EMI and Marconi, smaller companies, have both adopted this pattern more recently. Before the 1960s they both had separate central research laboratories and development laboratories, which the divisions used. They abandoned this structure because of the associated problems of technology transfer (Marconi: 'Central laboratories made no contribution'; EMI: 'Interface problems').

Differences are to be observed between the three companies in their methods for fostering innovation. In RCA there is a management system for assisting technology transfer. Development teams from the product divisions are allocated to the central laboratories to finance new developments in the divisional development laboratories. In EMI the problem of technology transfer is 'recognized' and they say that they have a policy for moving personnel from research into development and production to get new ideas accepted. They have eliminated the paying of higher salaries in research since 1964. They are trying to develop a *system* for ensuring the success of the policy and agreed that getting people to move was a problem. Management now evidently gives high priority to moving developments fast from research through production to the market. In Marconi the reorganization of research in 1962–67, decentralizing development to profit centres, took place because they saw that ideas could be wasted. The central laboratories, after all, had made no contribution to their efforts in colour TV.

124

CONTRASTS IN THE EXTERNAL ENVIRONMENT

The environment facing the three companies differed in that RCA was able to a greater extent to influence the public body with responsibility for colour TV; as the owner of one of the two major US television networks it had a favoured starting position; it was not largely influenced by government fiscal policy and the market itself was richer and ready for colour TV earlier.

RCA was the principal competitor with CBS for the approval of the Federal Communications Commission (FCC) to develop a colour system. As the potential manufacturer of the whole system it could direct an unremitting attack on the FCC to get its system accepted. Marconi and EMI were only tentatively engaged in considering a full system and would not be likely to be chosen by the broadcasting networks to develop a full system unaided by other companies.

RCA had a favoured starting position for two reasons. First, it owned the NBC networks which was an immediate and tied outlet for its equipment; this left RCA only the job of convincing the sponsors and the public. Second, it was a major manufacturer of domestic equipment itself, even though obliged by law to license competitors. Marconi and EMI had no tied outlets and no consumer divisions by 1960, and thus had a less strong position from which to lead development. Moreover, the BBC, which before the war had given imaginative backing to EMI, at first was in no hurry to go over to colour from monochrome and then was dominated by concern to achieve worldwide compatibility – which in its eyes meant the US system. In practice the differences between PAL and SECAM have been less troublesome than was feared, but they do pose problems for receiver manufacturers and administrators.

Fiscal policy in the USA, to the extent that it did affect sales of consumer durables, was not a direct threat to RCA in that it affected only part of RCA's sales. In Britain the separation between consumer and capital goods manufacture meant that makers of radio and TV receivers were more vulnerable to the vagaries of fiscal policy (in the form of HP controls and purchase tax); so few were willing to risk development capital on colour TV.

America in the 1940s and 1950s was a much richer society; colour TV for the whole population was a possibility in the 1950s, even if it did not start to become a fact until the 1960s. In Britain, monochrome TV for all was established only by the early 1960s, and colour will probably need 10 more years.

125

REASONS FOR SUCCESS OR FAILURE

Colour television, at first sight an apparently obvious case of European failure and American success, is as difficult to assess as any of the innovations discussed in these studies. It is not really possible to say that the British or Europeans failed and the Americans succeeded. One must analyse performance into failure or success in achieving specific objectives. Viewing the situation in 1945, one might have set out possible objectives as follows:

(1) For the company: (primary) to develop a full colour TV system and get it accepted by as many nations as possible; (secondary) to develop at least part of such a system, compatible with the main techniques accepted and sell it on the commercial market; (tertiary) to manufacture part of a colour TV system under licence and sell it.

(2) For the broadcasting organizations: (primary) to put into operation a technically satisfactory colour TV system on a nation-wide basis; (secondary) to have a degree of compatibility with the systems of other nations which would make possible the transfer of programmes and the transmission of international programmes.

(3) For the nation: (primary) to have available a colour TV service; (secondary) to dispose of national R and D resources in an economically efficient way.

All these of course are subject to a proviso of being generally profitable; we could not get full information on this from the companies.

The American success consisted in achieving the primary company objective. The RCA system is in general use in the USA, although SECAM and PAL are improvements on it. But the USA has partly missed out on objectives 2 and 3 (a successful broadcasting service for the whole nation). The US system is more difficult to operate and gives less consistent results because it does not use the PAL system for stabilizing transmission. The secondary objective (compatibility with other countries) has not been achieved. As far as the national objectives are concerned, the primary objective of having a TV service is attained, but it is worse than the European one (even though most Americans may not realize it) because it was too early, quite apart from the difficulties of a system involving some 800 stations and transmission of programmes over long distances. The Americans have probably missed out badly on the secondary national objective (economic use of R and D) because RCA had to start its work too early, before the market was ready, and sustain it through a long unprofitable period.

EMI and Marconi achieved only the secondary company objectives (developing part of a system) but, given the companies' own decisions to abandon their consumer interests, we believe that this was a sensible decision on their part in the circumstances at that time (they abandoned full system development about 1952–53 and camera work in 1960–64). They have resulted in all four broadcasting and national objectives' being fully achieved.

To recall why they opted for a more limited objective it is worth looking back at a key period, immediately after the war, when RCA started its work on colour. The American economy then enjoyed a much higher level of consumer incomes. To the British companies there seemed to be little prospect of selling colour television, and so they delayed their efforts to develop a system until about 1948–50, when RCA and CBS were already competing for FCC approval. Both Marconi and EMI started some work on colour in their central research laboratories at that time and decided on general lines of development. That they decided to go no further in 1952–53 is explained by the companies in the following terms:

(1) They did not have the £30 million which it might easily have been necessary to spend to develop a full system. This was about equivalent to the whole turnover of EMI and probably more than double the turnover of Marconi.
(2) Even if they could have raised the money, the market was not ready and they would have had to carry the investment for 15 years.
(3) RCA was far enough ahead for them to have little prospect of catching up with a competitive system.
(4) In any case, to use the same basic system in Europe and the USA was more sensible. They were not afraid of RCA's competing in Europe because the company, as an old subsidiary of Marconi, had always been prepared to leave the European market alone and had wide-ranging patent use, licensing and knowhow agreements with EMI and Marconi.

Whether these reasons are accepted as sufficient or not, and we think they were at that time, there was another period at which crucial decisions were taken, even if only by default, not to develop a full system or improve the RCA system in Britain. This was in the early 1960s, when it was becoming increasingly clear that Europe would be starting colour transmissions in the late 1960s. Marconi and EMI were the two British companies with most experience of colour TV, but both of them decided to go ahead on only one very limited area of development: cameras and some other studio equipment. In neither company does it appear that any wider system development was seriously considered; therefore there is no assembled schedule of the reasons for not doing so. However, for the companies, the retrospective case for their decision by default might run as follows:

(1) The NTSC system developed by RCA was pretty well established in the USA and was almost certain to be available to Europe: developing a competitive one was too difficult commercially and crazy technically. Compatibility would be lost. Developing a variant which was compatible would be thought merely nationalistic – being different for its own sake.

(2) The two main companies, Marconi and EMI, had given up their interest in electronic consumer goods in the 1930s and the 1950s respectively (for reasons which are implicit in the items below), and thus they felt that their interest in colour TV lay only in developing cameras (the transmitter is anyway very similar to the monochrome transmitter). The domestic equipment market was felt to be unattractive and unrewarding.

The companies which were actually in the business of manufacturing receiver sets were, of course, trying to develop colour receivers. But their effort was directed at the minimal level of improving on the NTSC circuitry, rather than at improving the basic system to avoid colour loss and picture fading. Although we were not granted interviews by the British receiver companies we approached, we have put together from other contacts a group of reasons to explain why they did not make the improvement eventually made by Telefunken.

(3) Capital for development was very short in the industry. The radio and TV side of many of the companies was not making money and the level of profit was not high enough to put money into colour TV.

(4) The situation had been caused partly, according to the industry, by 'stop-go' controls, particularly of hire-purchase charges on radio and TV, resulting in a very unstable market situation – and a particularly low ebb in the 1961–62 period which was important in colour TV development. One might add more generally that the

slower overall growth of British incomes made it hard to finance large-scale development.

(5) Further, the relationship with the Government (or the authorities) was also extremely bad because of indecision over the transfer to UHF and 625 lines and the introduction of colour. This meant that domestic TV manufacturers did not foresee a stable future for the product.

(6) There were also technical factors. To produce a good PAL system you had to have a storage ultrasonic delaying device, and this was too expensive in the earlier stages. Telefunken, through its wider interests in capital goods, was in the right position to make use of a cheaper version at once.

The criticisms of these arguments which we could put forward are as follows:

Although the NTSC technology was established, everyone in Europe agreed that it should be improved. There was little excuse for not trying something of the PAL type because everyone knew that it had earlier been suggested in America by Haseltine Corporation. The capital goods companies could probably have found capital (nothing like as much as would have been required for a new system). The receiver companies could have been more realistic about the market. The crucial failing in Britain seems to have been that capital goods companies and receiver companies were always separate, which was not true of Telefunken. Apart from bringing together capital and marketing ability, a company in both fields could also have been more likely to tackle the crucial storage delay device with a wider technical expertise. In getting out of receivers the capital goods companies were betraying a familiar tendency in some British industries: to be weak on competitive markets where commercial skill is essential, and to prefer technically oriented fields where competition is less fierce.

It should be added that the development of yet a third European system (in addition to PAL and SECAM) might not have been in anyone's interest. Indeed, if there is any general moral to be drawn from the case of colour television, it is this: here is a classic case of the large-scale, technological system most easily developed in a large company serving a large, publicly controlled market, an archetype of the reasons of scale which have given technological leadership in some key fields to the USA in the past 20 years. Such considerations do not exclude smaller companies and nations from getting a profitable slice of new technology markets, as Marconi and EMI showed in this case. There will, on the other hand, be major cases in the future where similar considerations of scale carry great weight. Wide-band telecommunications are one of these. In such cases a European programme by public authorities and Europe-wide companies, may be essential, if the risks and advantages of leadership are not to fall again to the United States.

Chapter 9

NUCLEAR POWER: AGR AND
BWR–A QUESTION OF STRUCTURE

Organizations visited:

Atomic Energy Authority (UK)
The Nuclear Power Group (UK)
Atomic Energy Commission (USA)

The technology of both the British advanced gas reactor (AGR) and the US water reactors had, in a sense, military origins. The US boiling water reactors and pressurized water reactors were developed originally to drive submarines and aircraft carriers. For this small reactors were needed; thanks to its weapons programme the USA had abundant quantities of the appropriate enriched uranium fuel. Westinghouse, for one, learnt its trade in the submarine business which rocketed up, like so much of US military spending, from the year 1955.

Britain's Magnox gas reactor programme resulted from its wish to have a plutonium production pile based on natural uranium to provide fissile material for atomic weapons. Natural uranium was an essential base for a country which wished to have some independence from American supplies. The piles, built at Winscale, used air rather than water as a coolant; water requires enriched uranium whereas with air natural uranium can be used.

The takeoff into peaceful power supply happened first in Britain where the Trend report in 1955 called for a major power station building programme to make Britain independent of imported fuel. In this period, 1955–63, while four Magnox power stations had been commissioned in Britain, very few were ordered in America, because nuclear power was still not seen to be competitive with conventional fuels.

At the same time, however, two other things were happening in America. The US Atomic Energy Commission was placing development contracts for a wide range of experimental reactor types in industry, both in America and, in partnership with Euratom, in Europe. And under the driving leadership of Admiral Rickover,

K

Westinghouse was settling down to building scores of reactors for the submarine and later the aircraft carrier programmes. US industry, in other words, was acquiring formidable experience and building up component manufacturing facilities on a large scale.

In 1963 the breakthrough into large-scale peaceful nuclear power began in America, when General Electric contracted to build at Oyster Creek a power station which would produce power competitive with conventional means. The tender was almost certainly, intentionally or unintentionally, a gross piece of loss-leading. GE was said in 1969 to have lost $50 million on this $80 million power station. The effect of the loss-price tender was dramatic. Orders for nuclear power stations of the light-water type rocketed and at the end of 1967 US industry was committed to build stations to provide over 40,000 megawatts. The market abroad has been swept by US reactors too.

The US development increased the pressure on the British to try to improve the performance of their own reactor line. The Magnox reactors have, on the whole, proved extremely reliable, with less time lost through faults on maintenance than their American rivals. But the Magnox system has one disadvantage compared with water reactors: the use of natural uranium with a graphite moderator leads to a physically large size and high capital cost. The fuel cost is much lower, but does not fully offset the high capital cost.

The AGR was simply an attempt to improve the fuel rating and to reduce the size of the reactor with the minimum degree of change to the technology, i.e. by enriching the fuel element. Work on the AGR began in 1956 with the idea, originally, of developing fuel elements clad in beryllium; these would require very little enrichment. Beryllium turned out to be unsatisfactory, but fortunately costs of enrichment were falling at about this time. The AEA was able to go over to steel-clad fuel elements. A 30 mw prototype at Winscale was sanctioned in 1958 and went critical in 1962.

In 1965 the first AGR nuclear power station, Dungeness 'B', was ordered by the CEGB after a competition between the design and American types of pressurized and boiling water reactors, designed by the British nuclear consortia under licence from GE and Westinghouse.

The decisions to develop and then try to build the AGR were not without their critics. In the early 1960s some argued that a more highly rated Magnox would be more competitive than an AGR. Critics argue that the AEA's hopes for AGR were based on beryllium and that, when this proved impractical, the economics became worse.

132

The contest, it is argued, between BWR and AGR for the Dungeness 'B' power station was 'cooked' – and so on.

Actually, it will never be possible to reach a final conclusion on all these arguments. Atomic Power Construction's winning tender at Dungeness 'B' has certainly escalated. But so, in practice, have the costs of the Oyster Creek power station on which TNPG's losing tender for a water reactor was based. It may be that, as TNPG argued, if the effort that was put into AGR had been put into Magnox, the cost would have been lower by the late 1960s. But who is to know? Conceivably, if the AGR had been developed and pushed by American companies with the same *élan* as they have devoted to water reactors, it, and not water reactors, would be sweeping world markets today.

Though this kind of back-jobbing gets nowhere, two facts, however, stand out:

(1) The AGR is being beaten in the markets of the world today on price – not by huge amounts, but by the order of £5 per kw or under 5 per cent of generation cost. TNPG, for instance, lost on price a contract in Belgium in 1968 in competition with a water reactor, and the same has happened in other cases. It may be that in special cases (for instance, Bayer, where process steam may be used in a chemical plant), AGR would have an edge. And one can argue, perhaps, that if reliability and operating costs were calculated more accurately, or differently, the prices would look different too. But in general the outlook for AGR, in terms of the price the market recognizes as competitive with PWR and BWR, is poor. The French decision in 1969 to go over to water reactors appeared to seal the fate of the first generation of gas reactors.

(2) The first AGR power station in Britain did not get built as early as it should have done, and this adversely affected the reactor's chances in world competition with PWR and BWR. Controversy surrounds the question of whether the consortia were pressing for the construction of an AGR power station in 1958 (that is jumping the prototype stage), and of what would have happened if such an idea had been implemented. But two other facts are not open to dispute. First, the Winscale prototype (built between 1958 and 1962) did fall between two stools: it was more than an experimental reactor, but it did not provide the real commercial conditions for fuel testing provided by a full-size power station. Second, there is no doubt that two further years were lost

133

between 1963, when the Winscale prototype came on full power and Oyster Creek was ordered, and 1965, when the CEGB ordered the first full-size AGR at Dungeness 'B'.

In 1963, TNPG believed the AGR was not economic and proposed development work to overcome the difficulties on fuel life, can thickness, fuel rating, can temperature, gas pressure and so forth. It argues that if that work had been done, a realistic tender would have been possible in 1965. But it was not done and Dungeness 'B' has both run into difficulties and escalated in cost. In retrospect, a double question is posed: why did not the AEA either place contracts with the consortia for the work or finance and undertake it themselves?

During the soul-searching in the industry which took place in 1968 (the Report of the Select Committee on Science and Technology – the Government's own reappraisal of its structure), the consortia made other technical or commercial criticisms of the AEA: 'They [depending on who is in charge] do not give them information effectively on certain reactors'; 'They did not take up TNPG's proposals to develop a 36-rod cluster for the AGR in 1963, and made them change to 18, and then found after all that 36 rods were needed for Dungeness 'B', and gave the job to APC.' Other criticisms of the AEA made by the consortia were: 'They build lavish test rigs for general purposes costing twice as much as a company with more precise commercial aims would spend'; 'By flogging a dying horse, the AGR, they are preventing a more lively and potentially competitive one [HTR – high-temperature gas reactor] from getting into the race.' And so on and so forth. The relationship sometimes seemed to resemble that of a maturing and increasingly restless student with his highly expert but paternalistic professor.

The two points – price, and faults of delays and decision-making – oblige us to look more closely at

(a) the economics of competition between AGR and BWR, and
(b) organization.

ECONOMICS AND SCALE

There is no doubt that the American effort in water reactors has cost a lot of money. To quote Milton Shaw, AEC director of reactors (in 1969): 'The AEC has spent more than $2 billion on civil light-water plant technology, and the industry has spent about $8 billion more to bring the light-water plants to their present stage of development.' Actually the US Government's $2·4 billion was mostly spent

134

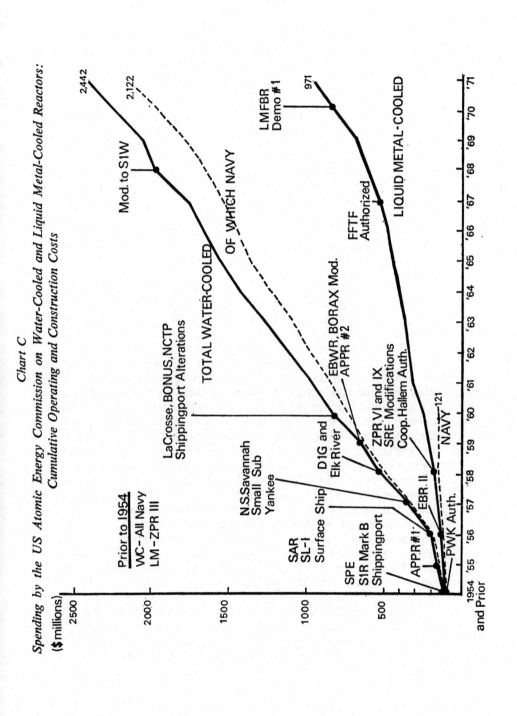

Chart C

Spending by the US Atomic Energy Commission on Water-Cooled and Liquid Metal-Cooled Reactors: *Cumulative Operating and Construction Costs*

under the naval programme (see Chart C); the effect was the same –
to spend money in the main industrial companies on reactor development.

By comparison the UK Atomic Energy Authority was spending
about £30 million each year on its entire programme of reactor
development in the late 1960s, of which about £7 million was on the
AGR. If the entire spending on the development of Magnox was also
included, the total, over the years to 1969, would come to £330
million. The three British consortia each spent under £1 million per
year on development; other development work was commissioned by
the Authority or tied to a particular power station.

The large spending by US companies of course includes large
investments in capacity for manufacturing components, working
capital and prototypes. The fact remains that they spend a great deal
more than their British rivals.

A look at the number of QSEs involved, however, reveals a different
picture. Before the hiving off of reactor development into industry,
the UK AEA employed 1,500 QSEs on reactor development out of a
total of 4,500 (and a total manpower of some 40,000). In 1969 the
US AEC employed only some 275 QSEs in its division of reactor
development and technology out of its total staff of 600. One reason
for this reversal of the financial disparity is of course that the AEC
does not undertake reactor development itself. Its task is to guide,
discipline and monitor the development work under contract in US
industry and in the power stations they are building, notably
through 25 QSE site representatives, who settle permanently on a
site and seek to establish a relationship with the contractor as a direct
representative of the division of reactor development and technology.

The major US effort, in terms of qualified manpower, is in the
companies. GE have not given us a breakdown of their development
team, but we put it in 1969 at some 600 QSEs, plus back-up – say
a total manpower of 1,500. Westinghouse employ some 600 QSEs plus
supporting staff, on the PWR, breeders and fuel, and another 1,300
QSEs on naval work for the AEC. In other words, the number of QSEs
directly employed in civilian reactors in GE, Westinghouse and
other companies, and the AEC (2,275), was roughly equivalent to
the numbers in the AEA and consortia in Britain (2,300), together
with 300 QSEs on nuclear work in the UK parent companies. As the
CEGB probably employs at least another 200 QSEs (annual nuclear
research some £2 million), perhaps as much as the US utilities, the
United States seems to employ as many qualified men on civil

136

Table 9
Estimated Total QSEs on Reactor Programmes (1968)

	Civilian	Military reactors
USA		
GE	600e	1,000e
Westinghouse	600	1,300
AEC	275	500e
Other companies	800	500e
Total	2,275	3,300
UK		
AEA	1,400	
Consortia	600e	
Companies	300	
Total	2,300	

(e = estimate)

nuclear research and development as Britain. The big difference is in the military field, where both the AEC and GE and Westinghouse have a massive additional boost. And this boost of course extends onward from development into production, where a large-scale component manufacturing industry has grown up, for instance, to serve the navy programme.

How can one explain the similarity in the scale of effort in terms of QSEs on civil work, when America's orders for power stations are so much bigger? First, America's QSEs in nuclear power are at present very fully stretched by their huge workload. With the UK power station programme fluctuating as it has, British consortia have had bad patches of under-employment. Then, a fair number of the British QSEs have been engaged in duplicating, or complicating, each other's work. In the case of the AGR, for instance, the basic design, and a good deal of continuous paternal guidance, came from the AEA; the consortia then improved and worked up the design in terms of detailed engineering; the CEGB in turn supervises construction and lays down remarkably detailed specifications to which the consortia must respond. The detail is such that when TNPG tendered a BWR for Dungeness 'B', based on Oyster Creek, GE was obliged to prepare a totally new and more complex specification. Finally, the companies do some component design.

In terms of research and development, after all, the US nuclear effort does not really cover a dramatically wider field than the British. It has explored a wider range of reactor concepts. But there are only three basic related reactors being applied commercially and a national effort in sodium fast-breeders. The extra amount spent in the USA over that spent in the UK (apart from higher salaries) is in manufacturing plant and working capital for actual power stations that are being built.

Thus in nuclear power, as in some other industries, the UK effort is over the minimum 'threshold' for a development effort. But that effort is being spread over a much narrower market than the similar American one, which therefore enjoys evident economies of scale.

There are fewer economies of scale on the production side. For major units of the nuclear boiler, after all, these appear only if there is replication. But at this stage in the development of nuclear reactors, economies and price cuts are being obtained mainly by technical improvements in each successive reactor that is built – which cuts replication out. All the same, major economies of scale have been obtained in production of components. Even in Britain, at one time one firm made all the actuators and some 700–800 were needed for the stations that were being built.

Above all, the sheer size of the two major American companies has given them the financial strength to loss-lead and thus create their massive market. So far the nuclear power business in the USA is not profitable, and indeed the companies seem to be experiencing severe technical difficulties as they struggle to satisfy their bulging order books. But in the background, GE and Westinghouse (with turnovers of more than £3 billion and £1 billion) both possess the resources to buy their way into the market and over the difficulties. Light-water power stations have produced more than their share of technical troubles. But, as with IBM, the sheer size and financial strength of GE and Westinghouse have encouraged utilities to rely on them to sort the problems out. Despite technical mistakes they have marketing predominance. The big companies may continue to sell reactors without a profit for some time to come, calculating to make up for it by sales of fuel, which can be worth twice as much as the reactor during its lifetime. So long as the AEA controlled the fuel business in Britain the consortia were not able to compete in this way.

138

DIFFERENCES IN ORGANIZATION

No less important than the economic differences of scale were the differences in organization of the industry between America and Britain, at least until the restructuring of the British industry in 1969. In the USA the development of nuclear reactors for both military and civilian purposes has taken place in industry, especially in the two leading companies, facilitating the transfer of technology from R and D through to the market place, when boilers for power stations are actually built.

The AEC places development contracts in industry and acts as a kind of foster-parent of industrial capability. In fast-breeders, for instance, it has for some time been systematically placing contracts which build up component manufacturers' capability and develop experience in fuel and safety.

All this provides a fertile soil for the efforts of private industry when, as in the case of fast reactors, they decide that the commercial moment has come to put down their own development capital and push ahead as quickly as possible.

The principle of contracting development work into industry was laid down deliberately by Congress when the Atomic Energy Commission was originally created. It was carried a stage further when the navy programme got under way. This programme was run by a formidable government administrator, Admiral Rickover, who imposed rigorous contractual conditions and a tight and demanding schedule on the main contractors, Westinghouse. It was a tough tutorial for the companies.

Once the navy programme was well under way, Westinghouse began to sense the growing commercial possibilities and began to invest some of their own money in civilian development. Government came in with judicious development contracts – and utilities with what were in effect experimental power stations. The push from Government was thus complementary to the broad engineering skills these companies possessed.

A few key engineers were transferred across from the navy programme into the civilian one; thus GE's chief world salesman was chief engineer on the *Nautilus*.

The British system, by contrast, involved at least four separate levels of design responsibility. In 1953 Sir Christopher Hinton, seeing that Harwell was too academic to undertake industrial development, hived off the separate Risley reactor division, which has developed AGR, SCHWR and the Dounreay fast reactor. At the prototype phase,

139

bids for components were put out to industry, but the AEA actually carried out the construction work. Completed and tested designs were then licensed to the consortia.

Until 1969, however, design responsibility for a reactor like the AGR remained divided even after it had been handed over to the consortia. Thus, the AEA remained responsible for the basic physics data. But the consortia, who have done a good deal of development work – for instance on on-load fuelling, the concrete pressure vessel, the polygonal spiral fuel element and so on – are responsible for most of the engineering.

A further division of responsibility affected fuel. This was the AEA's province; yet improved fuel performance is the key to improved reactor design and, as we have seen, price competition in reactors can depend, decisively, on whether a competing company can expect to recoup losses on fuel and whether it can offer the security of a long-term fuel supply.

Then there is the interface with the CEGB, which seeks to supervise power station construction and modify designs in far more detail than American utilities. The CEGB can produce some justifications for its officiousness. A hundred CEGB engineers have been needed to put right the difficulties at Dungeness 'B'. But such troubles owed something to the debilitating effects of putting out contracts on the basis of 'Buggins's turn'. Certainly the CEGB's interference in design snarls it up, adds to the workload on a consortium, raises costs and further diminishes the sense of responsibility of the consortia.

Disadvantages of Britain's Former Structure
This British system of organization thus had the following disadvantages:

(1) Responsibility for reactor development and for the quality of a reactor system sold to a customer was divided – always a bad management principle.
(2) Communications between research, development and the market had to pass through four organizations, multiplying effort and diminishing commercial effectiveness and the feedback from the market to development.
(3) The talents of the impressive reservoir of brainpower in the Atomic Energy Authority were denied a commercial outlet and sealed off from the market.
(4) On the other hand, both the consortia and the companies, which

140

did live in the market place, were deterred from investing their own money in development work, because they felt that ultimately they sold to a monopoly customer whose demands were erratic, and that his buying policy and their own development policy were determined in large measure by the views of the AEA.

(5) Most important of all, despite the apparent competition between the consortia on detailed engineering design, their common dependence on the AEA for basic reactor systems and the general policy of not allowing tenders to the CEGB based on foreign reactor systems, meant that there was no effective competition in the *choice* of reactor systems.

The AEA can show that it has excellent internal management systems for making choices on the economics or technology of different reactor systems. But it cannot fail to be subject to the inherent pressures on a large monopolistic public body – like the desire to demonstrate that money spent on a particular established system (say AGR) had not been wasted, and that alternatives are less attractive. Moreover, the many controversies about the timing of the AGR's development are a reminder that there is room for a variety of views on such crucial commercial questions. The way to settle them is through competition between different reactor systems in the market place. That was shown in 1965 when the challenge of the light-water reactors spurred both the AEA and the consortia to make the AGR commercial fast.

So long as the consortia based their designs on a common reactor coming from a single source (AEA), competition between them was bound to ring false. The main virtues of competition in this field are when it serves to select the optimum system and the best firm from a range of fast-developing technology.

REACTOR DEVELOPMENT INTO INDUSTRY

To overcome these difficulties and the basic economic problems of scale posed by the giant American companies, it seemed clear in 1968 that any reorganization of the industry ought to obey the following principles:

(1) Development of reactors must in future be carried out in the same organizations as produce and market them, i.e. in industrial companies as in the USA.

(2) There must be more than one of these, in order to permit choice of and competition between reactor systems within the British

141

market, and in order to develop to the full international links with a variety of companies and reactor types.

The right aim seems to be to develop strong British components for, say, two major European groups which would have the strength and scale to compete effectively with GE and Westinghouse and which would be able, increasingly, to standardize components in their supply to the entire European market.

(3) These British elements of European groups should not be structured according to any preconceived existing pattern (e.g. two consortia), but should be encouraged to emerge round the best management teams in the British nuclear industry.

(4) The new enterprise must fit in with the need to conserve and make the most of British and European resources in the vital new generation of reactors, the fast-breeders, which will dominate the 1980s. Here the situation is characterized by the following facts:

(a) Britain's Dounreay sodium prototype is still two to three years ahead of all others.

(b) The AEC and American industry are putting on the pressure and are perfectly capable of overtaking Britain at the commercial stage.

(c) France has begun to build (and Germany plans to build) prototype sodium fast-breeders which will virtually triplicate Britain's prototype. The Europeans thus seem likely to spend in all some $1,500 million on triplicated prototypes of 250 to 300 mw which show every likelihood of being overtaken by American effort which could cost less.

(d) Though the odds are still on sodium, it may be important that Europe take out an insurance policy in a gas-cooled fast-breeder prototype.

The triplication of effort in sodium, however, must make it harder for governments to raise the $150 million that are needed to finance a joint European gas-cooled prototype, for which plans have been drawn up by OECD's European Nuclear Energy Agency (ENEA). In the USA, while the AEC is concentrating effort on its fast-breeder programme, it is also financing a modest gas-breeder development.

Work on a gas-cooled breeder would follow naturally on from work on the AGR and its logical successor, the high-temperature gas reactor (HTR), and ought, probably, to be carried out by companies working in this field.

The reorganization of the British industry, which finally crystallized in the early summer of 1969, appeared to fulfil some of these conditions, at least at the national level.

In theory, reactor development work is to be carried out in two industrial enterprises. One is The Nuclear Power Group, which contained the best team at the level of the old consortia; the second is British Nuclear Design and Construction, a new company formed from the nuclear enterprise of GEC, English Electric, Taylor Woodrow and Babcock and Wilcox. This group has the advantage of embracing development and manufacturing in a single company, as Siemens or Westinghouse do. In practice, the AEA continues to spend far more on reactor development internally than it does in the two industrial concerns.

The new structure of the British industry leaves many questions about the European future unanswered. Originally it seemed that the objective of British participation in two major European enterprises, each of which might pursue a distinct line of reactor development, would best be realized by (a) transferring the AEA's sodium fast-breeder team to the Babcock–GEC–English Electric group, since those companies had obtained most of the component contracts for the Dounreay fast-breeder, and (b) encouraging TNPG to concentrate on the gas-cooled line of development which had long been its major interest. Then each British enterprise might have formed part of a European group. GEC, however, under Sir Arnold Weinstock, was not willing to take over the entire fast-breeder team from the AEA. The sodium fast-breeder team has therefore been transferred to The Nuclear Power Group, which thus becomes Britain's strongest enterprise in terms of reactor development, with an interest in both high-temperature gas reactors and sodium-cooled breeders.

If industry is to become the main location for development of reactors, it is logical that it should be given the opportunity to share in the fuel business, through the new mixed company led by the AEA, British Nuclear Fuels. This too has a European aspect. It is in the fuel business (gas centrifuge and fuel processing) that joint European efforts have recently made most progress.

While reactor development will be executed in future mainly by industry, under development contracts from the AEA and using industry's own resources, much basic research will remain in the AEA. Facilities like the Springfield laboratories would remain in the AEA and be used as a common service for which industry would pay.

143

But it is important that the industry be free to commission research where it wants and in the form it wants and that, to the maximum extent possible, a commercial relationship be established between industry and AEA research laboratories.

BUILDING A EUROPEAN NUCLEAR ENTERPRISE

The first important steps toward a major European nuclear reactor enterprise were taken in 1970 when The Nuclear Power Group and Kraftwerkunion (Siemens and AEG's heavy electrical and nuclear enterprise) announced an agreement for joint marketing of the present generation of reactors. This means essentially that the two companies will not compete with each other in tenders to third markets and that they will together be able to offer in any market the light-water reactors (pressurized and boiling water) brought to the group by Siemens and AEG, and the AGR and SGHWR brought in by TNPG. In a market such as Finland, where TNPG is better placed, it will be they who will represent the group; in South America it will be KWU. Design work and production of components will be sub-contracted across to the partner company where appropriate.

The biggest savings, however, will be attained when future development work is also pooled. TNPG brings to the group considerable knowhow in high-temperature gas reactor technology. More vital still, TNPG and KWU are the natural partners for a common effort in the vital fast-breeder technology.

By early 1971, thanks to a series of postponements, Kraftwerkunion had not begun work on its 300 mw prototype, even though much development work had been done. If the two partners could agree on a complete pooling of their knowhow, it would be logical to abandon the German 300 mw prototype and move on together to construct a 600 mw plant, probably in Germany. The next step would be the construction of a 1000 mw plant in one or the other country.

For TNPG, such a move would mean sharing a precious technological lead. But it would also bring crucial advantages. By avoiding duplication both companies (and both Governments) would free resources which could be invested in further development and in the huge effort of applied engineering, marketing, and technical support necessary to exploit the technology on a global scale. The overall partnership with KWU should give TNPG the kind of broader engineering and sales support which the British nuclear industry has sadly lacked in the past by comparison with its American rivals. The partnership would add credibility to fast-breeders in an uncertain period when US rivals may dissuade buyers from pushing ahead, by talking fast-breeder reactors down, or would enable the Europeans to match the Americans if they decide to move. The link gives both companies a broad industrial and financial base and access to a wider market in which to fund their development work.

Is there a possibility of a second European nuclear group's emerging, in which BNDC (Britain's second reactor group) would play a part? A link with the second major German group – Krupp–GHH–Brown Boveri, which has a key position in the development of high-temperature reactors through its pebble-bed prototype – provides a start in this direction. Could this group develop links with France's nuclear industry and fast-breeder programme? When this book went to press the future structure of the French industry was still obscure. If fast-breeder knowhow were to feed into Brown Boveri's French subsidiary, the second European group would be well on the way. Is it possible that CEM, Brown Boveri's French subsidiary, will combine for this and with the French-owned Compagnie Générale de l'Électricité?

The strength of this second German group in high-temperature gas reactors makes it a natural candidate for an important role in the task of constructing a joint European gas-cooled fast-breeder prototype, an alternative line of technology which might be developed as an insurance policy in case the sodium fast-breeder proves unsatisfactory. A saving of funds by pooling resources in sodium fast-breeders might make it easier to invest in the gas prototype as well. Obligatory licensing arrangements would probably have to be imposed to ensure that companies not participating in sodium or gas-breeder prototypes could ultimately use whichever of the technologies sweeps the board.

Just what pattern the nuclear industry in Europe will take is still obscure. But one thing is clear. Just as the shifting of reactor development into industry is essential to emulate the good communications between development and market which are a key to US success, so the kind of combination that is developing between TNPG and Kraftwerkunion is essential to achieve the scale of development resources and the broad home market which were also responsible for the success of GE and Westinghouse. The gradual opening up of public markets for power station equipment within an enlarged EEC will help the full benefits of such combinations to be realized.

Chapter 10
OSCILLOSCOPES: THREE ROADS TO MARKET

*'... a classic case of the use of small business techniques ...
the main mistake was to try to enter the market by licensing
alone ... the sheer size of the US market has enabled successful firms to finance a large-scale continuous development
effort.'*

Companies visited:

Hewlett-Packard (HP) (USA)
G & E Bradley (GEB) (UK) Subsidiary of Lucas
Telequipment (UK) Subsidiary of Tektronix

The world market for oscilloscopes is dominated by an American
company, Tektronix, which we did not visit. Instead we studied three
companies which used contrasting methods to challenge Tektronix
and gain a market share.

During the Second World War the oscilloscope began to be used
widely as an analytical electronic instrument. The model which
was probably most commonly employed was called the 339, made by
Cossor. These were fairly cheap instruments with what was even at
the time regarded as a poor performance; they could not calibrate,
were insensitive and had rather poor cathode ray tubes. Tektronix
is a company started by two electronics engineers after the war in
order to make better oscilloscopes. Being users of the instruments
they thought they knew what technical standard was required and
what price the market would pay for them. Their first instrument was
one with all the features which the Cossor 339 lacked, and was sold
at more than twice the price. The indications are that this was what
electronics engineers had been waiting for. Tektronix had early and
outstanding successes in the USA, though it took until 1957 for them
to set up a subsidiary in Europe (actually in the Channel Islands).

TELEQUIPMENT: A SMALL FIRM FINDS A SLOT
Before Tektronix had reached this stage, a similar entry into the
market was made by Telequipment. This company was started by a

TV engineer called Groom. He was a former employee of Standard Telephones and Cables who had done an apprenticeship and tried unsuccessfully for an external B.Sc. While at STC he had built himself an oscilloscope which he thought was better than the 339. Telequipment's original product, made in a 10-foot-square shed, was a pattern generator. The company took a stand at the 1953 radio and TV show and put the oscilloscope on the table as well to fill up space. By the end of the show it had attracted many inquiries and several orders. But the company did not produce this model because it was easier to redesign and produce a better job. The oscilloscope was deliberately aimed at the £50 range of instrument because they felt it was beyond their capability to make a sophisticated version. The market for oscilloscopes is very wide; you can get a £1,000 model to use in any applications, or a model at almost any price between that and £50 to perform a more limited function or with lower performance. This variety of product means that it is a very hard area to break into. If you only try to make one size of oscilloscope it has got to scoop the field in order to recoup R and D expenditure. Now that Tektronix is so well established an effort to compete across the board must come from a fairly large company.

It was lucky for Telequipment that it chose the £50 instrument, because there was a hole in the market at that level which Tektronix did not cover then. As the market for pattern generators fell away, Telequipment increased its sales of oscilloscopes. Turnover climbed much less spectacularly than Tektronix's and was only £250,000 by 1962. The second and third models of oscilloscopes were in the same range, but models selling at up to £250 are now produced as well. At the end of the 1960s Telequipment's main product cost £75 and held 80 per cent of the British market for the type excluding the Services. Of the previous model, 20,000 had been sold. Telequipment did not manage to expand because of credit squeezes at times when orders were very high and facilities should have been extended. In 1961, when delivery dates were very long, some competition was felt from Solartron which picked up sales in the £100 instrument area. EMI, Marconi Instruments and Nagard also tried to enter the market at this stage, but did not succeed. In 1966 Tektronix took over Telequipment and its products now slot into the Tektronix range.

G. & E. BRADLEY: LICENSING ALONE IS NOT ENOUGH

G. & E. Bradley is as unlike Telequipment as it could be. Started as a repair and calibration shop for Marshall Plan equipment in

L

1948, it entered into design and production of electronic counter-measure devices, microwave equipment and calibrators in the 1950s. The company tried to enter the oscilloscope market in the early 1960s. It appeared that there was a gap for an instrument costing about £120, run on batteries and using transistor technology. Given a good instrument in a popular range, about 5,000–10,000 units per year might be sold in the British market; the company thought that for such an instrument, selling at £120, there should be a market for 2,000 given that it was the first one they had made. Allowing a 15–20 per cent profit margin, of which half (10 per cent of sales) at most could be spent on R and D, the maximum R and D effort would be £20,000 or the cost of three QSEs plus support for one year. They were not sure that the work could be done for this price. When the sales manager found them a licensed instrument of the right type they decided to enter the market with this instead of developing their own. The licence was bought from a French company, Ribet Desjardins, and a cathode ray tube was bought from Telefunken. The oscilloscope was put into production and a number of orders were obtained, but when the first batch was completed they could not be persuaded to function properly. The licensor company was called in, but admitted that it had experienced the same trouble; before the instrument was licensed to GEB it had only been operated in a development version. This was an expensive and almost disastrous experience for GEB, which only redeemed its name slightly by taking instruments back and redesigning them from scratch, then putting them out as a totally different model.

This company has since showed that it is capable of learning from mistakes. It has designed and marketed successfully and profitably a battery portable 20 MH_3 oscilloscope (the 150) which is at least as good as any of the known competition and is superior in pulse handling capability.

HEWLETT-PACKARD: FAST GROWTH IN THE LARGE US MARKET

Hewlett-Packard is a company started by two engineers before the last war to make electronic instruments. It is a very successful example of the engineer-led, technology-orientated, fast-growing company. Turnover by 1969 was over $300 million, with a labour force over 15,000, so turnover was $20,000 per man whereas GEB in Britain could only manage about £2000 per man; Telequipment, an unusually successful small British company, achieved £4000 per man.

By 1964 Hewlett-Packard had become a serious competitor in the oscilloscope market, even though Tektronix was so well established that it was very hard to get into the market. For a big company like HP there is no point in aiming at anything other than a high volume area of the market; this is the philosophy which allows them to grow at about 20 per cent per annum and still show a gross profit of about 15 per cent. But Tektronix have 20 years' experience in the field and a new entrant would probably have to spend more than Tektronix initially on R and D, just to produce an oscilloscope as good. That would mean that, even if the product was as successful as the Tektronix one, it would probably have a lower net profit margin. It would amount to the new firm's 'carrying' the instrument until they had wiped out the difference in design experience.

The strategy HP thus decided to adopt was to try for an instrument rather ahead of the one Tektronix seemed likely to produce next. Even if the result lacked the refinements of long experience, it could be hoped to have an edge in technical advance. In the early 1960s HP attained a lead in 'sampling oscilloscopes', a special kind for examining ultra-high and microwave frequencies. In 1966, as the culmination of a 2-year development project, the company introduced a general-purpose laboratory oscilloscope intended to be somewhat ahead of the one Tektronix was expected to produce next. We were unable to get information about its sales volume or market share from HP for commercial reasons, but general opinion from other people in the 'trade' is that it has added considerable strength to HP's position in the oscilloscope market. According to HP it has also attained a satisfactory return on R and D, as measured by the method of calculating return factor, described on p. 152 below.

APPRAISAL OF THE COMPANIES

Of the three companies attempting to secure a viable position in the oscilloscope market, Telequipment succeeded technically and were able to do something which Tektronix could not do. But commercially they have been unable to achieve a growth record comparable to that of HP or Tektronix, and their merger with the latter company was aimed at securing more capital for development. G. & E. Bradley did not succeed technically or commercially at their first attempt, even though they may have retrieved the position. HP fulfilled its expectations commercially and technically.

Telequipment is almost a classic case of the use of small-business techniques in building up a successful company. Basically it is a single-product organization. There is no research done (not surprisingly in a company with only 300 employees) and very little development either. What the company really does is to design and engineer a workmanlike product. Before 1969 they were not employing any QSES. There was nothing up to that year which could be called a development programme. The process of project selection (or choosing which product they would make) consisted of little more than spending a few minutes discussing a drawing with some of the personnel who were going to produce the new instrument. Because the technical effort was so rudimentary, Telequipment could make money in this rather small area of low-value instruments. Tektronix had tried to get into this market, but was unable to gain a share of it because the product they developed was of too high a quality.

This failure by Tektronix was one reason for the takeover, a deal containing advantages for both companies. They had been in touch with each other for about 8 years before the merger and had developed a healthy respect for each other's different technical skills. For Telequipment the attraction of this deal was that it would have no more problems in finding capital and that Tektronix would provide a powerful US marketing outlet. Capital had been mainly needed to expand production facilities, but it seems likely that they will now start to spend slightly more on a technical programme. Since the merger they have started a development engineering section. In spite of its expressed need for capital at the time of credit squeezes, the company had done nothing about seeking it before 1966 other than arranging a bank loan of £5,000 at one stage. The main reason was a desire to stay independent of accountants and financiers, even though they are quite content now to be allied with another technology-oriented company. The Telequipment management continue to run the company. It is possible that they might have borrowed money from NRDC if they had asked for it, but given NRDC's terms Telequipment's management feared this would have reduced growth even more because it would have diverted capital needed for investment in plant.[1]

WHERE GEB WENT WRONG

The main mistake which G. & E. Bradley made in entering the oscilloscope market was to try and do so with a licence alone. It is almost

[1] NRDC arrange loans on a basis of repayment as high as they think the product will bear. This is because they have only a fixed sum to lend and want to increase it.

always true that the attempt to licence a product without having any independent R and D effort in the field, results in severe technical problems. It is difficult enough to do without independent R and D when buying a licence plus knowhow, when the licensor sends a team to help start up production. It is even more difficult to make a product merely from somebody else's technical drawings. The difficulty occurs because the licensee is unable to assess the technical standard of the product he is buying; he does not know what the key areas are which will determine success or failure for his production operation; and he has no knowledge with which to sort out production problems.

GEB did not understand how difficult the market was before they entered it. Their decision to licence was based on sales estimates, which did not appear to justify an independent effort. They did not, however, make a correct appraisal of the cost of the development effort needed to manufacture under licence. An organizational mistake was made when the introduction of the instrument was handed over to the post-design services group and not to the development laboratory. These mistakes have been rectified in the case of the subsequent 150. The decision not to go in for one of the high market-volume oscilloscope ranges was determined by GEB's lack of capital. As a subsidiary of Lucas the company is required to be self-supporting for capital needs in development and investment. Lucas was always prepared to bail GEB out if the company got into the red and needed to waive dividends to finance development, but it was not willing to provide additional finance for development. As a subsidiary GEB could clearly not go to the stock market. Banks required a security and would only make short-term loans. The NRDC's terms were very uncertain and GEB were required to give assurances about markets and profitability which there was no basis for forecasting.

HEWLETT-PACKARD: CLASSIC SYSTEM

Hewlett-Packard went about the business of developing oscilloscopes in a classically systematic way. Their general philosophy is that they are a company manufacturing electronic instruments for a commercial market, not a defence company doing exotic applications of new technology for the Government. Consequently there is a reluctance to work to any defence or government department specifications and they do not feel that this is a good way to maintain standards – you do a better job if you have to form your own. Instead of taking service specifications they synthesize the service requirements with what their other customers are asking for, add their own judgement

151

and aim to build something they can sell to anyone. In some circumstances they do work for the services; this tends to be at the pure end of the spectrum where the technology has widespread applications.

The R and D budget tends to run at about 10 per cent of sales, which level they think is necessary to keep the growth rate at 15–20 per cent and profits at about 8 per cent after tax. This latter figure results from a calculation of the return factor on a product development. They estimate that the life of the average product provides 5 years of earning power and the return factor is calculated thus:

$$RF = \frac{\text{5-year profit}}{\text{R and D cost total}}$$

Ideally this should be as high as 5 – in other words they strive for a profit each year as high as the total cost of R and D. If the average development time for a project is 2 years, then you expect the year's profit to be twice the R and D budget (i.e. a 20 per cent profit on turnover is twice the 10 per cent spent on R and D). In fact there is a lag from year one to year three at least, and the average R and D of years one and two should be half the profit of year three. Using a model of this general approach, but in more complex form, HP developed an overall sales and R and D strategy for the new product.

HP's main sales force includes more than 300 field sales engineers (all technically qualified). These people do the day-to-day selling. There was a time when each was expected to sell the full range of instruments to any customer, but with the rapid growth and diversification of the product line, some specialization is appearing. Throughout its history the company has always placed strong emphasis on its marketing and sales effort.

In addition, in the corporate staff there is a group called Technical Services, which reports directly to the president. Among its functions is product development planning, which includes the review of all R and D projects and their co-ordination with each other and with marketing.

R and D is done at two levels, the corporate research laboratory and the divisional product development departments. The former has a staff function and relationship to the divisions; the latter have a line responsibility in the divisional organization. In HP Laboratories (the corporate R and D department) the emphasis is on advanced research and they employed about 125 QSEs in 1970. Their budget was about \$4·5 million in 1970 (out of HP's total R and D budget of about \$30 million). Generally speaking, HP Laboratories

152

are allocated resources equivalent to roughly 1·5 per cent of sales, while the divisions get 8·5 per cent.

HP Laboratories have a responsibility to do research on new products, generally up to the stage of demonstration of feasibility. Then they pass the project to the division which is most responsible for that particular line to complete the development. HP Laboratories generally do not undertake the final development or tooling of new products, but if none of the divisions can take on a particular new development because it is too elaborate for local facilities, or because it is too remote from their product lines, then HP Laboratories may continue the work up to production tooling. Eventually a division has to take responsibility at the production tooling stage.

Transfer of Technology

In each of the successful companies we have visited we have taken a special interest in the transfer of technology between market and development. In HP this is encouraged by the fact that QSEs tend first to be recruited into sales engineering, and then to move back into production and development. Sales engineers do not have time for systematic market research, but they do feed back a consensus of customer needs, and this forms both a measure for existing development projects and a background against which those initiating new development projects assess what they think the customers will need in 2 to 3 years' time. A second important measuring rod for new requirements is the company's own use of instruments. When, in the course of their work, HP Laboratories find themselves making and widely using a new instrument, the engineer who has made it may then get the job of developing the instrument into a commercial product.

The environment in which Hewlett-Packard lives – the mass US market – has a further favourable effect on the innovation process in the company. Because there are far more customers, many of them sophisticated, there is a bigger feedback of new ideas than in, say, Britain. Because the customers are many it is possible to make a much better general assessment of future needs, not biased by the arbitrary accidents of a few key customers' requirements. And of course the sheer size of the market and therefore of sales and production has enabled successful firms like Hewlett-Packard and Tektronix to finance a large-scale continuous development effort to introduce new products and enhance the old.

Sources of ideas for new products, in a typical division such as

153

microwave, are 20 per cent field engineers, 30 per cent internal and 50 per cent marketing strategy. The latter means making estimates of the expected life of an instrument, what degree of advance can be incorporated into the next model and where the right price should be fixed. Ideas for wholly new products originate more frequently in the company's laboratories. Wherever the idea originates, two classes of information usually contribute to the selection of new projects: engineers' awareness of measurement needs (synthesized from the market) and the inputs of knowledge they get about new technology from HP Laboratories and their own projects. The combination of the two may generate a new idea. The customer is less likely to do this because he does not have the technology input. He is inclined to see only the immediate need of the moment, and what must be done now to beat the competition, but some pattern can be discerned from his requests.

Manpower

Hewlett-Packard is an intensive user of QSES – about 10 per cent of its total employment is in this category. Key factors in its use of QSES are:

(1) Virtually the whole of the company 'establishment' is technically qualified.
(2) QSES are well paid and keep pace with top executive jobs if they are good.
(3) They are encouraged to have independent ideas and are given an allocation of time to evolve new instruments.
(4) The more academic are usually involved in more advanced projects (i.e. Ph.D.s work more often for HP Laboratories) but there is no suggestion that they can go ahead on an innovation which does not appear to have large commercial potential. They are not allowed to feel they are following a hobby.
(5) Quite a number of the engineers have an MBA as well as technical qualifications.
(6) There is a high degree of control over the direction of technical development.
(7) QSE training continues even inside the company – through HP-sponsored classes and courses.

Hewlett-Packard feel that the crucial factor is to get the engineering right – that quality has to be built into the instrument from the initial design stages. They also believe that the best team to work on a

154

project need not include the people most expert in the field. Often some people from outside the field, providing they are technically qualified, can bring a new and fresh approach to difficult design problems.

Chapter 11
OLEFIN PLANTS FOR ETHYLENE PRODUCTION

*'One of our enemies is technological pride within the company;
it is nothing but a phoney nuisance.'*

Companies visited:
Stone & Webster and other plant contractors
Chemical companies

Before the war the developing organic chemical industry was based largely on acetylene as its raw material. Farbwerke Hoechst in Germany and Shawinigan in Canada both developed the earliest complexes which were based on carbide acetylene and gave rise, through organic synthesis, to acetic acid, anhydride, esters and chlorinated solvents.

After the war ethylene began to displace acetylene, partly because of the unstable qualities of acetylene, but also because of the steady development of cracking technology in the years since 1930, and the emergence of a large enough demand to make it economic to produce ethylene on a substantial scale by cracking other hydrocarbons.

The general development of cracking in the years between 1930 and 1945 had several origins. Refineries in the USA were raising the octane of gasoline under high pressure and producing light gases, such as ethylene, as a by-product. The war brought a massive improvement in metallurgy which was later to make possible the high-temperature furnaces (up to 700–800°C) used in ethylene plants.

In the USA the cracker stock for the growing ethylene production was ethane, and this continues to be so because of its availability in refinery off-gases and as a component of natural gas.

In Europe ethane was not available. In Germany, therefore, ethylene was produced until the mid-1950s by further reduction of acetylene; in Britain much of the demand for ethylene was met until 1951 by dehydration of ethyl alcohol, a relatively simple process in which there are few economies of scale. In the late 1940s, however, the development of plastics, especially polythene, opened up so large a market that it became economically attractive to develop ethylene

156

production by cracking naphtha, an oil fraction distilled from crude oil. This would have been uneconomic on a small scale but was potentially much cheaper if the scale was large. Moreover, naphtha, when cracked at high temperatures, yields not only ethylene but considerable quantities of other useful olefins and products. The co-products (which include propylene, butadiene, motor gasoline and mixed aromatics) make naphtha cracking economic, provided there is a ready use for them at high purity value.

THE OLEFIN BREAKTHROUGH: ECONOMIES OF SCALE

In the postwar years a number of chemical and oil companies in Europe therefore began to explore the development of naphtha cracking for ethylene production. They turned in the main to American plant contractors; these did not have significantly more experience than others in naphtha cracking, but they did have valuable American experience in refinery technology. The plants built then were a great deal smaller than those of today. ICI's first plant, for instance, completed in 1948, had a capacity of some 35,000 tons per annum. But as demand for ethylene expanded further, steady improvements in the chemical engineering of the plants brought dramatic improvements in their economic performance; ICI's latest plant, completed by Lummus in 1969, has an output of 450,000 tons. Plants of up to one million tons capacity are now planned in Japan. Table 10 shows how plant size reduces both operating and capital costs. It should be added that an even more dramatic reduction in capital cost per ton occurred in the earlier stages of plant development – between, say, the early plants of 50,000 tons capacity and those of 200,000 tons. Some plant contractors suggest that the capital costs per ton in today's plant of some 500,000 tons are as little as one-third of those for the earliest plants of 30,000–50,000 tons, while operating costs are also down, reducing total cost per unit of output to about a quarter of what it was 20 years before, without allowing for inflation. It is hardly surprising that there has been a massive increase in the output of ethylene-based plastics taking advantage of these economies of scale.

This immense improvement is due essentially to a steady improvement in the chemical engineering of the plant and an optimization of its scale and component parts. The growth in size of the plants made possible similar components of larger and more economic size (pumps, compressors). Sometimes a step change in design took place, as when the move was made from reciprocating to centrifugal compressors. The centrifugal compressor does not, like its reciprocal

157

Table 10

Olefin Plants: Effect of Plant Capacity on Production Cost, Naphtha Feed, European Location, Premium By-Product Value

Capacity, '000 tonnes ethylene/year	150	200	300	500	700	1,000
Costs, $/tonne of ethylene						
Feed cost	70·25	70·25	70·25	70·25	70·25	70·25
Operating cost	46·50	43·80	40·05	36·40	34·20	32·60
Sub-total	116·75	114·05	110·30	106·65	104·45	102·85
By-product credits	(76·00)	(76·00)	(76·00)	(76·00)	(76·00)	(76·00)
Production running cost	40·75	38·05	34·30	30·65	28·45	26·85
Depreciation on investment	34·00	30·85	26·90	22·90	21·00	19·50
Total production cost	74·75	68·90	61·20	53·55	49·45	46·35

Source: J. W. Gibson and W. Tucker of the Lummus Company in 'Large Plants a Sound Economic Proposition', *Financial Times*, 5 April 1971.

predecessors, require overhaul every few hundred hours. This made possible the construction of plants with only one compressor, a major saving in capital cost. Optimization also meant achieving the smallest number of furnaces compatible with, say, one furnace's coming off-stream for maintenance without cancelling out the economic benefits from larger plant.

Thermal efficiency is a critical factor in ethylene plant. The cracker operates at very high temperatures, the refinery at low ones; optimizing heat transfer between these two parts was therefore a vital part of the learning process.

Computer control is essential to performance of the plant. The cost of the system can be as much as $2 million; since virtually the same computer system can be used for a one million-ton plant as for a 450,000-ton plant, economies of scale are important here too.

In short, 20 years of continuous engineering development work throughout the world has brought a radical improvement in the economics of the plant.

Today there are signs that the technology is levelling out. ICI's next plant is likely to have a capacity of 600,000 tons. In Japan, one chemical company has placed a contract for construction of a one million-ton plant; further refinements, like larger furnaces, will improve the economics; efforts are being made to reduce further the time off-stream for maintenance. Some diseconomies of scale are, however, beginning to appear. For instance, parts of the plant are becoming so large that they have to be assembled on site, but in general the slowing down of the returns from larger size means that further breakthroughs will depend on more basic innovations – like a better catalyst for the cracking process or a shift in the relative economies of various feedstocks.

The major chemical and oil companies throughout Europe have all bought large plants, to enable them to share in the booming market for this basic chemical material; some eight million tons of capacity had been installed in Europe by 1970. To provide the ethylene necessary to meet the forecast demands in the 1970s, estimates suggest a need to erect in the Western world between 10 and 15 ethylene plants each year, and each of the major contractors will be setting their sights to capture as much of this business as possible.

During this period there will be emphasis on increasing the yield not only of ethylene but also of butadiene and of aromatics. There may well be a gradual move toward use of 'gas oil' as an alternative or replacement feedstock and a continuation of the developing

159

techniques of transporting ethylene by pipelines and sea-going tankers.

RELATIONS WITH THE PLANT CONTRACTORS

The plant contractors are the basic designers of olefin plant, but the customers – the chemical companies – must be in a position to evaluate their proposals, monitor their work and feed into it the lessons of their own experience and requirements.

This task is a substantial one. By the time a bid reaches the stage of a detailed submission (by which time the number of competing contractors may have been reduced to two or three) the cost of a bid may reach some £50,000; it may consist of a roomful of paper. In a field such as ethylene plant the contractors are expected to fulfil the company's requirement but to innovate where they can and maintain a continuous dialogue with the purchaser during the design and erection phases. Purchasers have to consider not merely the paper price and specification, but also the contractor's workloads, their experience of this size of plant and of the feedstock, their likelihood of reaching the required level of efficiency, the type of operating guarantees offered and which team the contractor is planning to put on the contract: in short, their credibility.

Once the contract is placed a close relationship between contractor and buyer is vital, with a continuous movement of engineers between the two and the purchasers perhaps undertaking special studies of new features.

The design and development of naphtha-based ethylene plant is thus a matter for the plant contractors, but it depends a great deal on a feedback of information from the chemical companies concerned.

THE CONTRACTORS

In the last 20 years a number of companies have emerged which are capable of building olefin plants of modern technological design to suit the varying circumstances of customers. These companies are each competitively evolving improved techniques, deeper cracking, improved metallurgy and greater energy integration, leaving the purchasing companies free to choose on the basis of their own detailed evaluations, requirements and judgements. The British subsidiary of the American plant contractors, Stone and Webster, had started an ethylene plant from naphtha as far back as 1946; so did Petrocarbon, a subsidiary of Manchester Oil Refineries. But Petrocarbon, through financial difficulties, was forced to sell out to the Finance Corporation for Industry in 1948, and this technology did not get developed by the new owners; their ethylene plant is reported to have become profitable by about 1952–54, but their technical position was eroded by the dissipation of patents and the development company was eventually liquidated. When the company was revived later, they did not return to ethylene plant except to provide some design studies for a Humphreys and Glasgow contract to East Germany which was never finalized. In the 1960s Humphreys and Glasgow designed and built three ethylene plants of their own design in Eastern Europe, but using the clients' cracking furnaces. They have not, however, won contracts in Western Europe or elswhere outside the iron curtain.

Plant contracting in Europe in this field is indeed dominated by the three major American contracting firms and the lead has fluctuated between them. Stone and Webster took the lead in about 1958 on the 60,000-ton range. They had built 60,000-ton furnaces in the USA (with ethane feedstock) and were in a good position to transfer the technology. In the early 1960s, the two other American contractors took more orders on the 150,000 to 200,000-ton range, partly because Stone and Webster's capacity was fully loaded, but Stone and Webster have since recovered their leading position. They have a larger European subsidiary (in London) than the other two firms and appear to do rather more of their design work in Europe.

Table 11

Ethylene Plants in Europe
(capacity in '000 tons completed by 1970)

Contractor	Tonnage	(of which UK)
Stone and Webster	4,168	1,380
Kellogg	800	380
Lummus	2,700	450

By 1970, 450,000-ton plants were being built and five are already in operation in Europe. Stone and Webster acquired their experience in this range by building a semi-commercial pilot plant which is operated in collaboration with Shell. Lummus obtained comparable experience by a similar arrangement with Japan.

A number of European firms are, however, successfully challenging these three American leaders. The German firm Linde, for instance, can build a plant competitive with those of the three major US

161

contractors. Lurgi have built two or three plants. European enterprises such as Linde in Germany or CTIP in Italy tend to be helped in acquiring a foothold by invisible national preferences and links with the local chemical industry. But Linde's engineers have also built a strong technological position which is beginning to make them a challenge in third markets. Their way into the business has been instructive. While the American companies acquired their essential foothold from their experience in refining technology, Linde based their entry on their skills in refrigeration derived from handling liquid air. Cold equipment is important in the refining part of an ethylene plant; Linde combined this skill with furnace technology for the cracking part of the process through a link with Selas of Philadelphia.

THE STRENGTHS OF US PLANT CONTRACTORS

The weaknesses of the British plant contracting industry have in the last few years caused a good deal of critical ink to flow. In what follows we do not intend to follow suit, but to try to illuminate the industry's problems by examining the reasons for the success of the American firms in this particular field.

Roots in Refining Technology

The US oil industry was the first major process industry to recognize that chemical engineering contractors could design and build refinery process plants better and more cheaply than the individual oil companies could. This resulted in the establishment and growth of the US contracting industry. In the UK there was only a small amount of oil refining before 1945 and the British contracting industry was small and based on the gas industry. The tradition in the chemical industry was that the chemical companies carried out their own research, development and design of processes, and even plant construction. Advances in refinery and subsidiary processes were usually associated with US industry, and British companies adopting these processes used US contractors who already had experience with the particular type of process plant. This is still true today. For British invention and development – e.g. the ICI reforming process and ammonia production – British contractors, given the opportunity, proved that they were capable of handling the engineering and organization of large contracts.

A second historical handicap for British plant contractors was educational. Until about 1950 British companies would have been

162

unable to recruit more than a few British chemical engineers. Although a few university courses in chemical engineering were started before the war, it was not until after the war that most universities began such courses; the present yearly output of graduates is about 700. This historical handicap cannot, however, be taken too seriously today, for most of the engineers in the strong UK subsidiary of a US firm such as Stone and Webster, are British.

Size

To compete successfully in the plant contracting business, a company must achieve a certain minimum size. International chemical companies demand internationally operating plant contractors, who can build them plants all over the world – and pick up the latest in technology from a world network of engineers. The British market alone would not be of sufficient size to sustain an optimum development effort in a major plant such as ethylene, where a plant now costs £25 million to build and can form part of a complex costing £100 million. It is of course the chemical companies which usually carry the bulk of this financial burden; even some of the largest US plant contractors have resisted ICI's pressure to buy such large plants on a turnkey basis, because of the financial risk, and ICI has found that the lack of dialogue with the contractor can create problems for the chemical company too. Nevertheless, even the engineering work on a single plant can absorb say 200,000 engineering manhours, or the work of 110 skilled staff in any one year. A company which wishes to sustain a balanced workload, with work on several plants backed by a continuous development effort, must achieve a turnover of some £10 million. Of the business won by Stone and Webster's UK subsidiary, 80 to 90 per cent comes from abroad.

The scale of effort required is shown by the manpower structure of the US plant contractors in Table 12, all of which have a comparable balance of skills. About 25 per cent of the manpower of these plant contracting firms are QSEs; the addition of staff with minor qualifications brings this up to 35 or 40 per cent in many cases. The second UK plant contractor shown, with 200 employees, is evidently too small to meet worldwide competition in such a field as ethylene plant. The first in the list has a manpower structure and a size very similar to those of the US companies. But as our report has shown, no British plant contractor is at present a serious contender in ethylene plant. Size, in itself, is not enough.

M

One other aspect of size is of course financial strength. The three main US plant contractors are all subsidiaries of larger conglomerates. The link gives these firms potential access to larger funds. They must, however, show that their development work is profitable, if they are to borrow from the parent companies to finance it.

One of the most important ways for the plant contractor to avoid excessive financial burdens is to reject the kind of damaging contractual terms (turnkey contracts which make losses, risky Middle Eastern oil contracts) which can bring heavy losses later. The company which is in the lead in technology and price can afford to turn down such business, which can later bring disaster. The risks for the inexperienced or improvident need underlining. On an ethylene plant costing some £15 million, the plant contractor's fee may be, say,

Table 12

Manpower in Some Plant Contracting Firms (1969)

	Total employees	QSEs	Other technical qualifications
US company I	1,500	400	150
US company II	1,600	410	100
UK subsidiary of US company III	570	108	43
UK plant contractor I	1,600	410	100
UK plant contractor II	200	60	20

£1 million. Of this, his profit may be £200,000–£300,000, a sum easily dissipated by bad forecasting or rash contractual terms.

In short, good project management and commercial instinct, applied to the latest known technology, are more important than hidden money bags.

Management Factors

The most significant factors in the success of the American plant contractors are indeed concerned with management. Let us look more closely at how these companies operate.

Although the plant contracting companies are advancing technology very fast, they are not involved in much fundamental chemistry; they tend to work very much at the development end of the spectrum. It is harder than usual to separate the development work they do from production because the companies concerned have little to sell except design techniques. Although they may build 20 plants of a similar capacity and basic technology, minor variations in each one to suit the customary special needs for feedstock efficiency and by-products, make each plant somewhat like a prototype. The companies are very heavily supplied with technical staff; they form about 35 per cent of permanent staff and are mainly engaged on a process which looks like development of plant. But it would be more accurate to say that they are really doing basic design, where each plant requires a large amount of design engineering at every level and in many disciplines. There is in the three large American companies also an R and D department, but it commonly accounts for no more than 1 or 2 per cent of employment and may not be easily distinguishable from the main 'engineering' group.

All the plant contracting companies interviewed were of similar basic organization. They resemble the development group of an aircraft company working on a prototype. At one end there is the research and engineering department, then the design department, then project construction and, linking them all, management and company services. There tends to be about a quarter of total employment in each area, except that 'services' might be less and 'projects' more to a complementary degree. Sometimes 'design' and 'project' departments are mixed together and sometimes 'research' is distinct from 'engineering'. Where 'research' is separate, it probably contains a higher proportion of Ph.D.s (perhaps half the total) and they are more likely to have chemistry degrees than engineering degrees. But whether 'research' is separate or not, it usually fulfils the same function of being a department of ideas, which are translated into fact through heat balances and energy equations by the process engineers in 'engineering', designed by the design department (i.e. pipe-work layout) and built by 'projects'.

Systematic Technology Transfer

In some German companies these departments are not distinct because the ideas men may be required to carry the idea right through to the 'on-stream' stage. In the American companies this is very rarely done and does not seem to be necessary because the process of technology transfer is carefully arranged and catered for by the company procedures. It seems likely that the American companies, having built up a lead in ethylene technology and thus having more work in the field, are able to make the frequent technology changes more a matter of routine. European companies

165

doing fewer plants are faced with a greater learning task on each one and thus have to adopt different methods.

Selection Procedures for Development Projects

The American companies have procedures for selecting development projects which can be explained simply. The system can be seen to be in operation and staff can see their own function and how to affect the decision, at what stage, if they think it is necessary. Thus, typically, one US contractor has a general rule that employees may spend up to 10 per cent of their time in following up personal technical interests; from this a new process may originate. Or it may come from a group of people in the research laboratory who have been set to work on a problem. In early development the individuals may take the decisions within this framework; where a series of tests and some equipment are requested the director of chemical research may authorize projects up to $4,000. Above that cost the planning group – a staff function of the research department – will assess projects and make recommendations to the vice-president of research. Initial suggestions most frequently come from sales people, who are all as highly qualified technically as anyone else in the company. There must be a formal assessment of sales prospects on any project above the 10 per cent level at each stage at which a decision is taken on it. At every stage a single individual and not a committee is responsible for the decision. He may get advice or recommendations from a group of people but he carries the can if it goes wrong. If a pilot plant is required (costing up to $100,000) it must have company approval.

Feedback from the Market

A crucial element in the process of development in the three American companies is the constant feedback of knowledge of the latest requirements and thinking of the chemical companies, as well as of world technical development. Sales engineers play a key role here; indeed theirs is one of the most important functions in any plant contracting company; in one of the three leaders, it was estimated that sales engineers spent at least half their time feeding back this advanced thinking from all over the world. It was a key task, too, of the sales manager, who also had the function of exchanging such information with the company's other major nucleus in the USA.

Another significant contribution to this company's development and competitive standing comes from the detailed reports from customers which the contractors ask for to explain the reasons for

166

failure, on the occasions when they do not get an order. Most such major customers are prepared to say why.

As one British manager in the successful UK subsidiary of a US plant contractor put it: '*One of our enemies is technological pride within the company; it is nothing but a phoney nuisance.* This feedback when we fail is a good antidote. It helps us to steer between our two goal posts – overdesign on the one hand (a constant danger) and missing out on the latest technology on the other.'

The feedback from the market place and from the world's technology is designed to get the plant contractor into a position where he can offer, not the most advanced process, but the most advanced *processes* – so that the contractor can offer the right solution to the diverse needs of customers. Feedstocks and conditions in Europe are more varied than in the USA. So they offer a greater range of technological stimuli as well as imposing a need for more flexible offerings from the plant contractors.

A constant dialogue with customers is essential when analysing the medium-term development of the market and hence future requirements. In the 1970s, for instance, naphtha will be in shorter supply; natural gas is producing new refinery products; lead-free gasoline will change feedstocks; and factors such as evolving technologies and metallurgy of pipes will produce further changes. The plant contractor must estimate the consequences of all this for his market and development programme.

Ethylene plant design has now settled down for the moment, but in the early stages a contractor's relationship with an individual chemical company was often crucial. Stone and Webster's pilot plant with Shell enabled them to obtain essential information about feedstocks and by-products which they could not have obtained in any other way. Lummus, by contrast, sold a furnace to BASF; unlike Stone and Webster they made no investment in the plant, so obtained back no information. Lummus have been obliged to build a pilot plant jointly in Japan instead.

The success of the US plant contractors in synthesizing information fed back from the market place suggests one of the reasons for their success in their approach to the customer. A customer going to an American contractor with an inquiry will get an advisory service on different plant types and technologies, comparing advantages. The options offered will have been synthesized from the contractor's worldwide technological reconnaissance system, will be backed by the contractor's own laboratory and may include his own processes.

167

One British plant contractor whom we visited seemed to work on the principle of asking the customer what he wanted and then offering to build it. The American approach is to try to offer him what he is going to need. We think the American approach, of seeking to know the customer's business as well as he does, is right. In this sector, the US plant contractors have placed the accent of their development work in the right place to yield effective commercial results. They have neither overspent energies on unregulated pure research into new processes, nor waited for the customer to tell them what he wants. Instead their intelligence system has constantly kept them in touch with the latest practical developments in technology; this they have synthesized so that they can offer the customer a choice of the best solutions to his needs.

The same kind of knack for making the best use of existing technology is responsible for the success of a firm like Dassault in the aircraft industry.

BREAKING IN

Is it possible for a European outsider to get into a race like ethylene plant when it is so far advanced? With plants of 450,000–500,000 tons being built and plants of 600,000 tons under consideration, there is a lot of experience behind the successful contractor's work; it is not easy to break in. Probably those most likely to succeed are enterprises like Germany's Linde or Britain's Matthew Hall which have a strong base in production of process plant and which then move into plant contracting, learning from the chemical companies as they go.

To succeed, however, and make such a business profitable, such enterprises must acquire an effective presence in a number of European and world markets and must make their presence felt when the major chemical companies are evaluating contracts; if they are to oust the firms with a well-established reputation they must, preferably, achieve some kind of edge in price or in a significant aspect of technology or perhaps be helped into the market by a degree of support from chemical or oil companies at home.

CONCLUSIONS

To sum up, American plant contractors dominate this aspect of chemical plant construction for the following reasons:

(1) They have longer experience of cracking technology from petroleum refining.

(2) Chemical engineering is a well-established discipline in the USA. It has developed more recently in Britain.

(3) The American companies provide a comprehensive advisory service on alternative processes and designs for the customer.

(4) The American companies also conduct more process development related to current technologies, but not solely for one contract. This means that they can offer customers new or improved solutions to their requirements, and options between different types of plant. Some British companies are merely prepared to build the kind of plant the customer asks for.

(5) The American companies have systematic processes for technology development and a well-organized feedback from the market.

(6) Their large domestic market gives them practice in transferring technology from development to individual plant design. It allows them to spread R and D over a larger number of plants.

(7) The American companies have sufficient financial resources behind them to sustain their development work. They are all part of larger industrial groups.

Should the dominant position of the US plant contractors cause concern to European policy makers? One economic consideration should be made clear. The plant contractor's fees and profits are a very small part of the total operating costs of the chemical industry, but their contribution to its efficiency is crucial. This is therefore a method of transferring management and technological skills from one country to another which brings large benefits but places a minimal burden on the balance of payments or economy of the receiving country. A mere 1 per cent improvement in return on capital on a £25 million ethylene plant would be enough to pay for the plant contractor's profit. In practice, between 1950 and 1970 the efficiency of ethylene plant has improved by several hundred per cent.

Chapter 12

NUMERICAL CONTROL SYSTEMS FOR MACHINE TOOLS: THE MAKING OF A MERGER

'Being out in front is burdensome, if development is not timed right to hit a market and cannot be matched by adequate investment in marketing and servicing.'

Companies visited:

Airmec ⎫
Ferranti ⎬ now merged (U K)
Plessey N C ⎭
Cincinnati (U S A)

The application of digital and analogue programmes to the control of machine tools has been one of the most significant innovations in manufacturing during the last 20 years. It makes possible rapid automatic operation of machine tools and precise control of complex tool operations. Used properly, NC can cut waste through scrapping, reduce the time taken in setting up repetitive operations, permit machining to accurate tolerances of up to 50 millionths of an inch, and ensure accurate repetition of complex operations. All this in turn cuts down the need for skilled manpower and makes possible better use of the skilled manpower that is available.

So far numerically controlled tools have had their major impact on the economics of batch production. In mass production it is not numerically controlled tools but automatic transfer lines and other fully automated systems which have so far brought the big benefits. But where batches of 10 to 50 components, say, are being produced, numerical control comes into its own, especially where accuracy is needed. In the production of aircraft wings or of large turbines, or of machine tools themselves, numerical control has brought major improvements in accuracy and efficiency. Its use has thus developed especially in capital goods industries and industries such as aerospace which have exacting machining needs.

170

NUMERICAL CONTROL SYSTEMS FOR MACHINE TOOLS

THE CONDITIONS FOR GROWTH

As with the computer revolution, it has been easy for armchair commentators and hopeful innovators to imagine a sudden revolution in manufacturing processes. In practice the introduction of numerically controlled machine tools has depended on the growth of a market which has in turn depended on at least four factors:

(1) *The cost of skilled manpower*: when is it cheaper to install a numerically controlled tool than to buy the skilled manhours needed to do the work instead?
(2) *The availability of skilled manpower*: when is skilled manpower so short that numerical control can close a gap?
(3) *Complexity of operations*: certain sophisticated machining operations are very hard to control by hand, or to undertake by other semi-automatic methods; they may be early candidates for numerical control.
(4) *Shop floor organization*: above all, the pace with which numerical control is introduced depends on the pace of change on the shop floor. Is management in a position to organize the flow of work so that fast-operating numerically controlled tools are fully utilized and pay?

Since all these factors – high cost and shortage of skilled labour, sophisticated aerospace requirements, management techniques (and willingness to work shiftwork) – were present first of all in the United States, it is hardly surprising that a large market for numerical control systems developed there first, in both the public and private sectors. Moreover, as in other advanced technologies, the American state played a major pump-priming role in the middle 1950s.

THE TAKEOFF IN AMERICA

In the very early stages of the technology European companies were as far ahead as the Americans. In 1949 the us Air Force and the Parsons Co., Michigan, jointly sponsored a programme of development at the Massachusetts Institute of Technology using a Cincinnati milling machine. Ferranti and EMI began work at about the same time. But in 1956, following the Korean War, the us Federal Government took the decision to build up a stock of advanced machine-tool capacity, both as a reservoir for potential armaments production, and as a means of stimulating advanced technology. The us Air Force approached the machine tool and electronic manufacturers, first with development contracts for numerically controlled tools and then with orders for batches of 50 – in all worth $30 million. Bendix, General Electric and Thompson Ramo Wooldridge (later Bunker-Ramo) obtained contracts for numerical controls and Cincinnati for tools. Software was further developed at MIT under government contract. Cincinnati, aware of the wider potential commercial market, soon attached an EMI-type numerical control system to its run of tools. This early EMI system was satisfactory, but the components were elementary (Post Office relays, for instance), and Cincinnati later withdrew them all from the Air Force and replaced them with an improved system. The incident was a revealing illustration, both of an early European lead and of the speed with which US development overtook it.

A crucial feature of the US development contracts was that they stimulated both machine tool development and control systems. Though numerical control systems were born in the electronics and computer industries, to work effectively they required important applied development work on machine tools. These needed, for instance, rigid spindles less prone to vibration, and hardened ways. Government development contracts helped to develop these and other novel features like automatic tool changing.

The years 1954–58 can be described as the years of development in the USA; a mere 173 tools were sold. From 1959, however, the commercial market took off, helped by the ability of both tool and numerical control suppliers to supply tools and controls already tested by the government market. By the late 1960s between 15 and 20 per cent of the value of machine tools installed each year in the US was numerically controlled. By 1969 some 19,000 numerically controlled machines had been installed in the USA, worth some £150 million.

THE EUROPEAN MARKET: FIVE YEARS BEHIND AMERICA

In the UK and the rest of Europe, by contrast, growth of the market was slower. In Britain the machine tool companies showed little interest until around 1960. Though shortage of skilled turners and grinders was apparent during the 1960s, a strong cost benefit, when comparing the cost of NC tools and manpower, was not apparent. Even today the estimated cost of ten years of one man's labour in Britain is only some £10,000–£15,000. In the USA the same amount of labour would cost over £30,000, or the cost of a numerically controlled tool.

172

In the early 1960s the aircraft industry in Britain placed some significant orders for numerically controlled tools for sophisticated aerofoil tasks, but the growth of this defence market was checked in 1964–65 by the cancellation of TSR2 and other aircraft projects. The British authorities placed only two development contracts with tool manufacturers that we know of[1] and neither could be considered a commercial success; none was placed on the Continent. By the end of 1964 some 547 systems (worth, say, some £5 million) were installed in Britain. The commercial market has grown steadily since.

On the Continent, the market did not start to grow seriously until 1965–66. Since then it has grown faster than in Britain (as Chart D shows). All the same, by 1970 the European market as a whole could be described as being at the same kind of level of development as the American market in 1964–65; that is to say, in France, West Germany and Britain, 5,160 machines had been installed by the end of 1969 (compared with 19,000 in the USA) and annual installations with numerical control were running at 10 per cent or less by value of new machine tools (compared with America's 21 per cent in 1969 and 9 per cent of shipments in 1964). In 1970 recession struck; it halved machine tool buying in America and cut it by 40 per cent in Britain; but NC should recover its position once the US economy recovers.

The relative weakness of the British tool industry in the first half of the 1960s should perhaps also be noted as an environmental handicap to British NC. In the next 5 years there was a big improvement. But according to OECD, the turnover of the British machine tool industry in 1967 was only £78 million, compared with £143 million for the stronger export-oriented West German industry. Thanks to the strength of the British effort in electronics and control systems, the value of British output of numerical control systems and tools was some £8·3 million, compared with £12·5 million in West Germany.[2] There is, however, no doubt that the British makers of

---

[1] The Fairey-Ferranti development of the first hydrostatic slideway machine tool in Europe (1958–59) and a Department of Scientific and Industrial Research contract to Staveley (1961–62) for one of the first machining centres.

[2] See *NC Machine Tools; Their Introduction in the Engineering Industries*, OECD, 1968. The OECD figure was far lower than the figure of £110 million for total home deliveries plus £46 million exports in 1967, given by the *Industrial Report by the Machine Tools EDC*, National Economic Development Office, 1970, but this defines machine tools far more widely. By the same definition, German output would be far larger too.

Chart D

The Development of the Market for Numerically Controlled Machine Tools

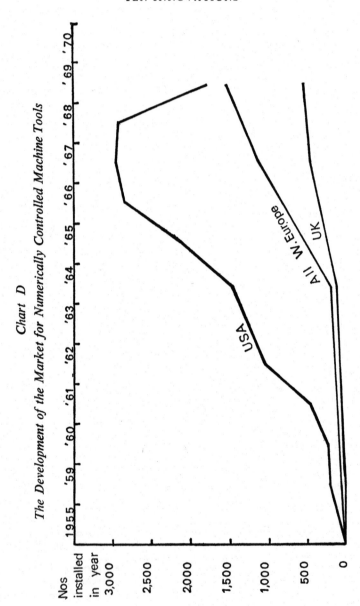

control systems would have been better placed if their own domestic machine tool industry had been larger and technologically more advanced, or if they had operated in a European market in which neither national sympathies nor tariff and other barriers inhibited the fitting of British NC systems to German tools.

The size, homogeneity and early development of the American market do much to explain why American companies lead the world industry in numerical control. Four companies, indeed, GE, Bunker-Ramo, Bendix and Cincinnati, the same four which originally obtained contracts from the US Air Force, share the bulk of the US market between them.

In a company such as General Electric, NC turnover in the USA and a significant turnover in Europe is served basically from two factories, in Virginia and Milan. By standardizing its product as much as possible it has achieved major economies of scale in production. We shall return later to this question of economies of scale.

AN AMERICAN EXAMPLE: CINCINNATI

The position of the Cincinnati Milling Machine Company is of special interest. It is the largest of the three US machine tool companies which develop and manufacture their own NC systems. Given the small proportion of the total machine tool market which uses numerical control (15–20 per cent in the USA by value and only 1 per cent of the number of tools installed), the market provided by one toolmaker is too small to support the cost of developing and manufacturing numerical control systems for all but the largest tool manufacturers. No European machine tool company has kept consistently in this race, though some have tried for a while. Cincinnati, however, with an annual turnover of some £100 million in tools has managed to do so.

It is worth pausing for a moment to look at Cincinnati, for it illustrates two things which were important for the development of NC: the high level of general engineering capability in the American machine tool industry, and the scale of research, development and servicing which the size of the US market made economic.

Cincinnati went into machine tools, originally, as a user. It was founded in 1860 to make taps and dies; when the company became dissatisfied with the milling machines available on the market, it built its own. Soon after, other users of milling machines noticed the Cincinnati ones and asked if Cincinnati could make further versions

175

to supply them. It has been in the business of milling and grinding (not turning) ever since, and is now the world's largest machine tool company, employing 13,000, of which 12,000 are in the USA, for a turnover of £100 million in 1967 (£7,700 per man).

At the beginning of 1968, 12 per cent of the labour force, or some 1,500 people, were graduate OSEs. Of these 1,500, perhaps 500–600 were involved in R and D and the other 1,000 in marketing and production. Research and development is divided between a central basic research department (231 people, of whom 106 are graduates), divided into three laboratories, and eight large design, development and engineering research departments in the product divisions. The central laboratories conduct research on machine tools themselves (driving methods, mathematical analyses of feeds, speeds, gear ratios and so on), and on physics and chemical problems such as cutting fluids, bonding, plastic mouldings and so on. The development departments design tools.

The largest divisional development effort is in the control division, dealing with numerical control systems, tracing and gaging systems and programming. This group has developed Cincinnati's NC capability. There are about 300 people employed in development and engineering in this division (covering both tool and control development), of whom about 100 are graduates. A further 300 graduates are employed in other divisional development departments.

Despite the scale of R and D in NC, the large turnover of some £20 million in NC tools and controls meant that it was only costing Cincinnati under 10 per cent of turnover in 1968; it was probably a lower cost than the effort going into servicing (though we were not given these figures). By the late 1960s, NC in America was characterized not just by a large market, but also by a strongly developed ability to apply NC to machine tools and large enough operations in the main companies to combine further research and development and large-scale servicing with profit.

European manufacturers have therefore faced American manufacturers who have had a head start, in terms both of scale and of continuous experience of a more sophisticated market. Their problem has been to time their entry, select their niche in the market and discipline their development work so as to avoid losing money but avoid missing the market too, as it rapidly emerged some 5 years behind the USA. In the following three sections we examine the routes taken by the three British enterprises which have now combined together in Plessey Numerical Controls.

176

TWO KINDS OF BUSINESS

Before looking more closely at the three British companies, a word of explanation is needed about the NC business. Numerical control systems are now being applied to virtually all the traditional machining operations (boring, turning, milling, grinding). Two main types of control are in use. One, the 'point-to-point' system, moves the tool to one fixed point (say where a hole is to be drilled), operates it, then moves it on to another point where a further operation is carried out. This kind of system is cheaper and is more readily applied to at least some types of conventional machine tools. The second type of numerical control system, the 'contour' system, moves the cutting tool, while it is operating, in a 'continuous path', and can be used for the machining of complex shapes. This type of control system is more expensive and meets some of the more sophisticated needs, in the aircraft industry for instance. Much larger numbers of the cheaper point-to-point machines have been sold, but the higher value of the contour systems means that the difference is not so large in terms of value. When assessing the route taken by three companies, the distinction between these two markets is worth bearing in mind (see Table 13).

Table 13

Sales of Contour and Point-to-Point Controls (1967)

	Numbers	Value of controls only ($ million)
USA: Point-to-point	2,050	36
Contour	621	27
UK: Point-to-point	330	3·6
Contour	140	4·1

Sources: US figures, OECD; UK figures, estimates from the companies.

THREE BRITISH COMPANIES

I. Airmec

Airmec is a small company whose ownership has had a chequered history but whose policy in numerical control has been consistent and, on the whole, successful.

177

Airmec was originally an electronic and laboratory instrument company. At one time it was part of Crompton Parkinson, at another of Philips. It settled down as a division of Controls and Communication in about 1960. In September 1967 Airmec merged with AEI's loss-making NC division to form Airmec-AEI (AEI kept a minority holding). A month later GEC took over AEI, creating major problems for the new joint venture. Sir Arnold Weinstock does not take easily to minority holdings, even in successful enterprises. In January 1969 the Racal Company took over Controls and Communications, Airmec's parent, and in August of the same year Racal bought out GEC's minority share. Finally, in October 1969, Plessey bought Airmec from Racal and merged it in Plessey Numerical Controls (PNC).

Fortunately, throughout this time until the final takeover, the Airmec management, led by Jack Varrall, the company's managing director since 1947, was remarkably stable, and in 1959, just as the British market for NC began to move, it selected its own way in. This was to develop and sell a cheap, simple, point-to-point control system, to catch the large cheap end of the market. During the development stage, in the year before introduction of the product, the engineering team consisted of three engineers with a little drawing office and model working support; this cost only some £15,000 in that year. About 300 of the Autoset 271 control systems developed were sold between 1959 and 1966, in the price range £2,000 to £2,500. From 1966 on, the Autoset 271 was succeeded by the Autoset 410 in the price range £2,250 to £4,500. The technology was still relatively simple to maintain and understand (it used Post Office relays) and continued to catch a substantial share of the cheap market (400 systems have been sold).

Throughout this period Airmec's NC business was profitable. This was achieved by undertaking only a relatively small amount of R and D, having small overheads (for production was built up initially in the same factory as the instrument business and carried to some extent by the same small-firm facilities), and charging the firm's servicing costs realistically. (The selling price included installation costs. There was an additional spares warranty of about 2·5 per cent and the customer was charged for any further special servicing.)

Though the Autoset 410 has sold well, Airmec discovered that as the market became more knowledgeable in the use of NC it demanded additional facilities which would ease machining problems and make machines more profitable. Airmec therefore began to plan for the

178

next jump in technology and capability; this it took in 1969 with the PTL100, a point-to-point control system which leapt semiconductor technology and went straight to integrated circuits. PTL100 involved an advance into a higher price range and sold in the range from £3,250 to £6,500, but like the cheaper Autoset, which continues to sell well, it is claimed to be the cheapest point-to-point system in the UK market and able to meet any price found on the European Continent.

With PTL100, however, Airmec was developing a different type of product from its original Autoset 271 and beginning to become a rather different kind of firm. PTL100 was basically an Airmec conception, but it was worked out, to some extent, by the AEI engineers who joined Airmec in 1967.

AEI had started to make machine control systems as far back as 1950, when it made a simple system for copying a template; it followed this up in 1955 with a control for a jig borer and in 1956, with Planetrol, a continuous path control system which in effect competed with the comparable Ferranti Mark IV. In 1960 it produced its Axiomatic point-to-point control system. It had also developed a small trace and readout system. By the end of the 1960s when it merged with Airmec, it had sold some £800,000 worth of NC equipment and was doing research and development worth £100,000 per year.

AEI's relatively slim sales in the more sophisticated end of the market do not appear to have been profitable and provided a return on its R and D. But even Airmec's R and D was costing it some £50,000 per year by 1966, as it climbed the ladder of technological sophistication.

After the merger the R and D effort by Airmec-AEI cost some £120,000 per year, reaching a peak in 1968–69 as PTL100 was developed. The development of PTL100 in fact cost Airmec more than it expected and pushed its NC business into the red for a year or two. By late 1969 it was approaching profitability again and breaking successfully into the new market for its more advanced PTL100 point-to-point system.

PTL100, however, taught Airmec an important lesson. Now Airmec no longer relied on its original successful niche in the cheap end of the market; it had also learnt that climbing the technological ladder can be expensive. It learnt too that introducing a more sophisticated product can involve difficult production problems and technical problems in applying the NC system to machine tools. For its next move ahead Airmec decided to take a licence from General Electric

N

of America, a world market leader. From GE it would have acquired lathe controls to supplement Airmec's own controls on drills, mills and borers and, later, contour controls.

Airmec in early 1969 was still a very small company, employing a mere 400 people for a turnover of £1·5 million including instruments. NC output was some £500,000 per year. Output per man, in other words, for the company as a whole was at the relatively modest figure of £3,750. The company used simple batch-production methods and kept profitable by paring down overheads.

Airmec's management were well aware by 1969 that a major improvement in production methods was essential to raise output per man. The licence from GE would have accelerated the process, enlarging the company's range of products and market share and giving it both the opportunity and the need to learn American methods of large-scale production. It would have been an important but not easy change of style for this small firm.

In October 1969, however, this story of successful development entered a new phase with the sale of Airmec to Plessey by Racal. The takeover was, if anything, a tribute to Airmec's success. Plessey paid Racal £2·2 million, a generous price, to acquire property and fixed assets worth £800,000 and goodwill put at £1·4 million.

II. Ferranti

The Ferranti company started development work on numerical control systems as far back as 1951, as a private venture. They had the largest electronic and servo-mechanical research and development team in Britain, financed by defence. They were looking for new commercial outlets for their R and D workers and chose the new field of NC. They were also concerned with seeing what electronics could do to overcome shortage of the skilled labour needed for their own large machining programme in the defence field. By 1956 Ferranti had produced a first saleable working device. Only one was sold, but in these first 4 years the company had spent £500,000 on development.

The Ferranti work was so far advanced that when the US Air Force first placed batch contracts in 1956, Ferranti were told that they were a year ahead of their American competitors. The orders were, however, designed to develop the American industry, so Ferranti was passed by. At home in Britain there was no comparable government programme and the private market, throughout Europe, was growing only slowly.

180

By 1960 Ferranti had spent £2·4 million on NC development. Of the leading NC producers, Ferranti was the only one in the world to use magnetic, instead of paper, tape; GE and Westinghouse had both given it up. Ferranti was concentrating on the more sophisticated market for contour equipment and getting about 75 per cent of the home market, in this narrow field. The only trouble was that the market had remained small. Even by 1963 Ferranti had still sold only some 150 control systems, half of them continuous path systems and half of them point-to-point. Total revenue by that date probably just about covered the £3 million so far spent on R and D.

Chart E

Plessey's Growing Market Share in NC

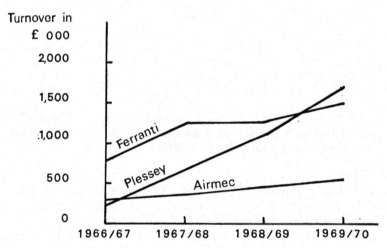

The market for lower-priced point-to-point control equipment for borers was, however, at last getting under way, pioneered by the Americans. Ferranti decided to try to get into it, at a level below Plessey's sophisticated Mark III (see p. 182). They did so with Scope, a point-to-point system in the price range £3,200 to £6,500. By this time Plessey had come in with its new Bunker-Ramo range and though Ferranti remained the market leader until 1968–69, Plessey was fast catching up, as Chart E shows.

In 1969–70 Ferranti was still spending a larger proportion of turnover on R and D than its two British rivals (it was still in the

181

most sophisticated part of the market); it was having difficulty, in consequence, in finding sufficient resources to finance marketing and the build-up of a service network – the key to a successful NC business – on the scale of its rival Plessey. Its management held the view that to be really successful an NC company needed to spend some £500,000 per year on R and D. At 15 per cent of turnover this would have required a turnover of some £3·5 million, but in 1969 Ferranti's turnover was still well below £3 million, compared with a total British market of over £4 million and a fast-growing market in the rest of Europe worth some £8 million.

In 1969 Ferranti tried to negotiate a joint venture arrangement with the German firm of Grundig, which had built up a successful small business in Germany in the same field as Airmec – cheaper point-to-point systems. This would have been a neat complementary partnership: Ferranti would have been given access to Germany, the largest market, and a strong servicing and sales network there, as well as entry to the cheap end of the business; and Grundig would have enjoyed complementary benefits in Britain. Grundig, however, decided not to go ahead with the deal (perhaps because it could not foresee as high a return on capital as in other lines of business).

In December 1969 the Industrial Reorganization Corporation solved Ferranti's problem in a different way by helping Plessey to buy its NC business for some £2·5 million.

III Plessey

The Plessey company decided to get into numerical control in about 1956. The work was organized at first as a sub-unit of the company's telecommunications division. At that time entry looked to be an expensive exercise, yet the market was still small. To find a market section which would carry the cost they decided to concentrate on high-accuracy point-to-point control systems, mainly for boring operations. They made use of the existing Farrand measuring system. Working with Alfred Herbert they developed a control system for the de Vlieg jig borer (made by Alfred Herbert under licence). This started a family of control systems designed essentially for the de Vlieg jig borer, which are sold partly by Herberts as their Datatrol and partly by Plessey for use with other machines. The current version of these, the Mark III, which emerged in 1965–66, provides at least three, and sometimes up to five, axis controls and many other refinements.

182

By 1964, though Plessey had acquired a reasonable share of the borer market, it became clear to them that there was little growth in this small sector and that they must find a way of diversifying into the wider NC business for controlling other types of tool. They decided to do so by taking a licence from an American company, partly on the classic ground that it is pointless to reinvent the wheel, and partly because the US market had developed first and therefore gave its manufacturers the feel for the most advanced needs.

Their first licence agreement, with Bendix (taken out in 1964), proved abortive. Communications did not seem to work. One problem was that most communications had to go through Bendix's patent office, and not direct with the NC division; another shortcoming for Plessey was that Bendix were willing to give Plessey an exclusive licence for the Commonwealth and UK only, not for Europe. Licence restrictions on markets are an important factor in NC, for if, say, Bendix had licensed a major German manufacturer, Plessey would almost certainly have been excluded in practice from fitting its controls on to German machine tools.

In 1965 Plessey switched and instead took a manufacturing and distributing licence from Bunker-Ramo, giving it the right to market these controls throughout the world outside the Americas and Japan.

The Bunker-Ramo range gave Plessey a wide coverage of the British NC market, except in cheap point-to-point systems dominated by Airmec. Bunker-Ramo's 3100 is a three-axis contouring system costing £7,000–£10,000. By adding extra options in the 3120, Plessey adapted it to more sophisticated needs in the £10,000–£20,000 price range. The Bunker-Ramo 3000 in the £15,000–£25,000 range provides still more advanced capabilities – suitable for complex contouring – and indeed can control up to 12 axes. Barely a dozen have been sold in Europe, all of them to the aircraft industry.

Plessey's NC business has been profitable for much of the 1960s, though it dropped into the red (like Airmec's) during the introduction period of the 3100. The Bunker-Ramo licence, however, backed up by a vigorous marketing effort, achieved its aim of rapidly enlarging Plessey's market share, as Chart E shows. By early 1969 they had passed Airmec and matched Ferranti in turnover. Plessey, however, had missed out on the cheap end of the market, which Airmec had so successfully exploited. They tried to take over Controls and Communications (Airmec's parent) in early 1969, but lost to Racal. In October 1969 they persuaded Racal to sell. The IRC's mediation and resources also enabled Plessey to take over the Ferranti enterprise.

183

IRC lent Plessey Numerical Controls £3 million at 4 per cent, rising to 8 per cent by 1974/75; the loan was to be repaid in full in 1974/75.

MANAGEMENT STRUCTURES COMPARED

How do the management structures and systems of the three companies compare? Airmec was run on small-business principles. That is to say, personal control by the managing director and a very small team round him, welded the different people in the enterprise into a purposeful team.

Plessey is run by a tight, strong, company-wide system of financial control and discipline. In particular, a rigorous system for controlling and monitoring research and development and its cost was installed in 1961.[3] Before any developments are embarked on, the sales department must have assessed the market for a product and drawn up a business plan based on an assessment of Plessey market penetration. The plan becomes the basis of a specification which in turn leads to a detailed engineering plan in which manpower, space and financial resources are carefully quantified. Production engineers are brought into this team to ensure that production considerations and value engineering are brought into the design from the start. Once a development plan is agreed and implementation starts, financial control becomes vital. It is maintained through a weekly monitoring of cost (via a computer programme), and monthly reviews of expenditure under the development programme and of its real progress. The purpose of this second check is not only to make sure that spending is matched by results, but to ensure that the timescale of development does not slip and miss the market. As with all such control systems, the most difficult point is the assessment of how the development is progressing. But at least there is awareness of this problem, close control, careful provision of cut-off points should the plan go wrong, as well as a close link between development and market.

Development in turn fits into the wider framework of Plessey's financial control system and company plan. There is a 5-year planning cycle, a total annual review and a partial review every 6 months.

The Ferranti company has a management style and structure of a more permissive kind. The company is organized on a divisional basis with each product/profit centre managing its own research and development.

[3] See W. Tulloch, *A Method of Controlling Design Projects*, a paper to the British Institute of Management, September 1968.

184

APPRAISAL OF THE COMPANIES

Airmec successfully carved out a niche in the cheap end of the market. Like Telequipment in oscilloscopes, it was in its early days a model of how a simple technology developed by a small firm can be made to pay. It paid, not only because the small-firm techniques (low overheads, simple communications) are economical, but because the product was well suited to the market – the unsophisticated organization of the British shop floor. By the time of the merger with Plessey and Ferranti, Airmec was discovering the need to extend its product range upward, spend more on R and D and improve its production organization. All this placed new demands on management and implied larger scale. One of the means chosen – a licence from GE – might have been successful had it been followed further. The takeover by Plessey was an alternative route and a tribute to success.

Plessey has been a successful example of how licensing can provide a base for wider advance, a means of containing R and D expenditure while building up a strong marketing organization and a strong market position, before acquiring a larger technological capability of one's own. Of the three British companies we have looked at, the company which has absorbed the others has been the company with the keenest eye for profit, the largest effort in marketing and servicing and the most rigorous and disciplined company-wide system of financial control. If the IRC helped Plessey to concentrate the industry, it backed the concern with the strongest management control system and the fastest-growing market share.

Ferranti demonstrated in the NC field (as in others) that European brains are capable of path-finding in a major field of innovation. It also showed that being out in front is burdensome in terms both of company profits and of national use of resources, if development is not timed right to hit a market and cannot be matched by adequate investment in marketing and servicing. Ferranti is the only company in the world to use magnetic tape for numerical and control systems; this has theoretical advantages, but there are practical difficulties too. Many smaller machine-tool users do not have the facilities for reprocessing it, as they have for the commonplace paper tape. So Ferranti provided a complete tape service, but that in turn placed a further premium on servicing. Once again we are reminded that sales of NC move no faster than life on the shop floor and that those who remain a small step ahead of its needs can often reap more rewards than those who make big leaps forward.

185

The lesson is apparent in many other fields of technology and indeed in the application of numerical control to whole systems of machine tools. The Molins company, for instance, has evolved the conception of a total system of machine tools, linked by computer, which will be programmed to manufacture a flow of components from beginning to end. In theory the process could bring enormous savings – in machining time, in stocks, in administration. For instance, in one example described by D. T. N. Williamson of Molins,[4] machining time for a batch of 12 complex components was cut from 206 minutes with a conventional machine, to 96 minutes with NC, to 12 minutes with the Molins System 24. In practice, however, though Molins has sold a number of individual machines out of its system, it has managed to persuade only one customer to buy a substantial part of its complete system – IBM. Most British engineering companies still organize the workflow through the shop by means of a tip from the labourer, with his truck, that Joe is running out of parts, or by bits of paper stuck on piles of parts. The pace of introduction of linked systems of numerically controlled tools will depend less on the development of the technology than on (a) managements' skill in reorganizing the flow of work, and (b) the extent to which those who supply such systems of tools can develop a complete consultancy and marketing service, which shows the customer how an optimal system can service his own specific needs and then supplies it to him. When one considers how long it has taken for companies to learn how computers might be of practical use in administration and management it is clear that a revolution in batch machining will take a long time.

Molins has thus run into one of the same difficulties as Ferranti: it is ahead of its time.

THE PROBLEM OF SCALE: THE MERGER

All three companies indeed faced a general problem, which can, to some extent, be compared with the problems faced by European computer manufacturers. There too the size and earlier development of the American market helped to give American producers economies of scale and a technical lead. The problem for European manufacturers was to enter, profitably, a smaller home market against US manufacturers who enjoyed economies of scale.

In the numerical control industry, Airmec, and to some extent

[4] D. T. N. Williamson, *The Pattern of Batch Manufacture and its Influence on Machine Tool Design*, James Clayton lecture to the Institution of Mechanical Engineers, March 1968.

Plessey, showed that it is possible to solve this problem either by finding a narrow untapped niche in the market and exploiting it (Airmec) or by licensing (Plessey) and building up the essential service and marketing network on this base. Both were finding, however, by 1970, that there was a need to offer customers a wider range; a niche can become obsolete. The trouble is that as a firm widens its range it finds itself burdened with the problem of high development costs, which strangled Ferranti. Paying for the higher costs requires deeper worldwide market penetration and larger investment in servicing and marketing to achieve it.

Table 14

QSEs Employed in Ferranti NC and Plessey NC

	QSEs (degrees)	ONC and HNC	Total incl. others
Ferranti (1968)			
R & D	39	37	101
Marketing, servicing	4	31	not available
Production and common services	7	64	not available
Plessey Numerical Controls (1970)			
Engineering	63	35	150
Marketing, servicing	10	63	170
Production and common services	not available		

The pressures of scale thus help to explain the merger. The new group, with a turnover in 1970 of some £5 million, spent £600,000 on R and D (or 12 per cent of turnover in that year). Table 14, which compares the use of QSEs and other highly qualified manpower in Ferranti and PNC, shows the larger effort in both R and D and servicing/marketing which PNC could afford. Even the new company, however, inevitably remains vulnerable to market swings. In 1971, the depressed state of home NC and machine tool orders meant that the £5 million turnover could not be sustained. In consequence R and D was drastically cut back.

Plessey also brings European and world market outlets which neither Ferranti nor Airmec possessed. Sales and service organizations have been set up in France, Germany, Sweden, Italy, South Africa and Australia, tapping into the facilities of the Plessey International Organization.

o

In theory, alternative ways of overcoming the problem of scale can be imagined. Airmec, for instance, if Plessey had not bid for it, might have made a success of a partnership with General Electric. Even without the IRC's intervention, Plessey might have been able to acquire Ferranti later at a lower price.

The later the merger took place, however, the greater became certain of the difficulties. Eighteen months earlier there would have been a good deal less overlapping in the development of new products. Airmec's PTL100, whose market overlaps with Plessey's NC22, would have hardly begun. Another new Ferranti development would not have had to be stopped. Once the merger has shaken down the group will be able to claim that they have a rather comprehensive product range; the reverse side of this coin is that a wide range of products, some of which are produced on a modest scale, is not the best way to achieve high productivity and economies of scale.

For PNC, success will therefore depend on how far it can enlarge its world market share outside Britain. Though PNC now has over 50 per cent of the British market, that is not a large nor stable enough base on which to build economies of scale comparable to those achieved by General Electric in the USA. It will be essential for PNC to win a substantial share of the European market which, by 1974–75, might be as large as the US market today – as European users tap the full potential of NC.

A major share of the European market can probably not be won merely by direct export. West Germany, for instance, is easily the largest manufacturer of machine tools in Europe, but German manufacturers tend, like British, to stick to national producers of control systems unless there are major advantages in the imported product. Certainly a powerful Europe-wide service network is essential to any company which hopes for a substantial share of the European market. Prizes may therefore go to firms in the numerical control business that merge or otherwise combine across the frontier acquiring a strong identification with the local scene in more than one country and rationalizing the production and development effort within their range between their different national locations. Ferranti's attempt to combine with Grundig and thus acquire a German base would have made very good sense if it had come off.

A strong service organization outside Europe is also important, for German toolmakers who export throughout the world want worldwide support, and this PNC does provide.

188

TOWARD COMMON STANDARDS

However successful a European company is in penetrating markets, its productivity will still be held in check by the variety of demands from the European machine tool companies.

One way of solving the problem is to reverse it and for the machine tool manufacturer to make his own control system as Cincinnati has done in the USA. Cincinnati holds the view that NC systems are best developed by machine tool companies because they alone have intimate knowledge of machine performance and needs.

The Cincinnati Company, however, is an exception. A number of European firms – Heller, Alfred Herbert – have ventured partially into the NC business but none has stuck with the policy on a permanent basis for the good reason that they were even less able than the electronics companies to achieve the minimum necessary scale – even if they had the technical capability in this new field. Probably the biggest difficulty for a machine tool company is to build up the world-wide servicing network that is necessary. Some machine tool companies claim to have just as much expertise in this field as electronics companies, thanks to their wide experience of working with different types of control systems. They argue, however, that to serve their customers' needs in different markets they need to be able to supply a variety of control systems. So the European business has been left basically to the electronics companies with the exception of certain firms, like Olivetti which started with a base in both tools and electronics.

How then can the excessive variety of needs in the European machine tool industry be reduced, in order to improve the efficiency and economics of the market for numerical control systems? There are several possible ways forward. One West German firm, Wotan, for instance, is attempting to standardize its own range of machines on to 4 main NC types (instead of 40) and would like to see a wider collaborative effort (with British and other European companies). At present, however, few machine tool firms may be willing to embark on a standardization which would clearly expose comparative prices. Wotan suggests agreement on optimum parameters for a certain type of tool, followed by joint efforts of development.

A theoretical alternative way of getting economies is for a major machine tool maker to tie up with a single major supplier of NC systems. Scharmann (West Germany) attempted such a tie-up with Philips, encouraged by a discount. But Philips were soon obliged to give the discount to others and the system broke down.

189

A more interesting European possibility might be for a group of machine tool firms to develop their own system or, say, take over or take an interest in a key electronics NC enterprise.

Again, however, there is no guarantee that such a system would prove to be the best or the cheapest, and both the machine tool group and the electronics enterprise might be inhibited by their ties in buying from and selling to others.

The main pressure for change may simply have to come from the marketing policies of firms like PNC: a firm such as General Electric of America has limited the range of variations which it will make for customers and imposed a certain pattern on the US market. One difficulty is that the main early source of expansion in the market must be the extension of the purchase of NC to smaller firms, and sales to such firms are often decided by minor features of the specification. Airmec partially overcame this problem by adopting a modular system of design and production. PNC will try first to standardize for different types of application.

During the next 10 years the European NC market will expand fast as Europe fulfils all the four criteria for a strong NC market described earlier in this chapter: high cost and shortage of labour, sophisticated machining requirements and better management. Small low-cost computers, performing some function of the present control systems, will play a growing part, as will larger computers grouping a number of tools together. The machine shop of the future will tend to be computer-controlled with conversational modes linking the production planning, scheduling and stores for materials and NC machines. By the late 1970s, one organization may well be the prime contractor for the supply and planning of equipment, machine tools, controls, computers and display devices. All this will enhance the value of the NC market in Europe. But economies of scale comparable to those in the USA will not be achieved unless the European market becomes more homogeneous. As in many of the other industries we have examined, achieving the successful application of this innovation in Europe requires both a continuing effort to create a single, open European market tomorrow, and adaptable and disciplined management in the real world of today.

190

Index

AEG, 144
AEI, 178, 179
AUDI NSU Union, 65
Acetylene, 156
Aero-engines, 61
Aerofoil, 173
Aerospace, 29, 170
Air pollution, 64, 66, 70–1
Aircraft: high-lift, 29; interceptor/ fighters, 36, 72; low-level, 46; manned, 36, 37; multi-role combat, 51–7; STOL, 37; single/twin engine, 38, 39, 40–1, 44; strike, 37–8, 51; supersonic, 35, 36; swing-wing, 35, 36, 40, 47; VTOL, 37, 38
Aircraft (variable geometry): Anglo-French, 38–9, 51; commercial effectiveness, 44, 48, 58–9; contractual system, 45–7, 56; costs, 35, 37, 39–40, 42–3, 46–7, 50, 55; drag problems, 29, 36; efficiency, 41–3, 53–5, 58–9; Europe, 39–41, 51–9, 116; France, 41–5; and government, 36, 42–4, 45, 47, 49–50, 51–2; growth, 35–9, 47; large firms, 11, 45; procurement, 43, 47, 49, 50, 51, 56; prototypes, 42–4, 47, 48, 50, 52, 53, 58; small firms, 6, 11; stability problems, 37; UK, 47–9; US, 36–9, 45–7, 58; wing design, 29, 36, 170; wing joints, 46, 52
Aircraft carriers, 46, 131–2
Airmec, 12, 177–9, 180, 183, 184–5, 186, 188, 190
Alberto, Jacques, 38
American Exchange, 8
Aromatics, 157, 159
Asahi, 93
Atar motor, 44
Atomic Energy Authority, 15, 136, 138, 140, 141, 143
Atomic Energy Commission, 14, 131, 136, 137, 139, 140, 142
Atomic Power Construction, 133
Atomic Weapons, 131
Auto Union, 62, 65

Automobile Industry, The, 67n.
Autoset control system, 178–9
Avionics, 46
Avions Marcel Dassault, *see* Dassault, Marcel (company)

BAC, 11, 26, 37, 38, 39–40, 41, 48, 51, 52, 53, 56
BASF, 167
BATS, 7
BBC, 119, 121, 125
BLMH, 10; *see also* British Leyland
BMC, 24, 86, 90
BNDC, 145
Babcock and Wilcox, 143
Baier, Professor, 61
Banking, 7
Barradell-Smith, Richard, 83
Batch production methods, 4, 13, 43, 45, 47, 50, 51, 52, 53, 55, 58, 78, 123, 170, 180, 186
Bayer, 133, 164
Belgium, 86, 133
Bell company, 36
Bell Laboratories, 96
Bell symposium, 6
Bendix, 172, 175, 183
Bentley Engineering Group, 7, 73, 74, 77–8
Beryllium, 132
Betts, Roger, 28n.
Billi stocking machine, 74
Boeing, 11, 35, 37, 38, 39, 40, 41, 43, 44, 45
Boussois, 90
Bradley, G. and E., 13, 147–8, 149, 150
Bristol (company), 47
British Aircraft Corporation, *see* BAC
British Indestructo Glass, 90
British Leyland, 24, 66, 89
British Nuclear Design and Construction, 143
British Nuclear Fuels, 143
Broadcasting (TV), 126
Brookings Institution, 17
Brown Boveri, 145

191